OBSERVING

SENIOR AUTHORS

Virginia A. Arnold   **Carl B. Smith**

LITERATURE CONSULTANTS

Joan I. Glazer   **Margaret H. Lippert**

Macmillan Publishing Company
New York

Collier Macmillan Publishers
London

ACKNOWLEDGMENTS

The publisher gratefully acknowledges permission to reprint the following copyrighted material:

"Amos and Boris" is from AMOS AND BORIS by William Steig. Copyright © 1971 by William Steig. Reprinted by permission of Farrar, Straus & Giroux, Inc. and Hamish Hamilton Children's Books Ltd., London.

"Bear Mouse" adapted from BEAR MOUSE by Berniece Freschet. Copyright © 1973 Berniece Freschet. Reprinted with the permission of Charles Scribner's Sons.

"Behind the Scenes of a Broadway Musical" is from BEHIND THE SCENES OF A BROADWAY MUSICAL by Bill Powers. Black and White photographs designed by Lucy Martin Bitzer. Copyright © 1982 Bill Powers. Reprinted by permission of Crown Publishers, Inc.

"Birds and Bears in Winter" is an adapted and abridged selection, pages 43–51, from SHIVERS AND GOOSE BUMPS by Franklin M. Branley (Thomas Y. Crowell) (text only). Copyright © 1984 by Franklyn M. Branley. Reprinted by permission of Harper & Row, Publishers, Inc.

"A Bowl of Sun" is from A BOWL OF SUN by Frances Wosmek. Copyright © 1976 by Regensteiner Publishing Enterprises, Inc. All rights reserved. Reprinted by permission of Children's Press, Division of Regensteiner Publishing Enterprises, Inc.

"A Box Full of Infinity" is adapted from A BOX FULL OF INFINITY by Jay Williams. Copyright © 1970 by Jay Williams. Reprinted by permission of Harriet Wasserman Literary Agency, Inc., as agent for the author.

"Cam Jansen and the Mystery of the Dinosaur Bones" is from CAM JANSEN AND THE MYSTERY OF THE DINOSAUR BONES by David A. Adler. Copyright © 1981 by David A. Adler. Reprinted by permission of Viking Penguin, Inc. By permission also of Scholastic Publications Ltd., Warwickshire.

"Digging Up Dinosaurs" is abridged and adapted and contains five illustrations from DIGGING UP DINOSAURS by Aliki (Thomas Y. Crowell). Copyright © 1981 by Aliki Brandenberg. Reprinted by permission of Harper & Row, Publishers, Inc. and The Bodley Head, London.

"Ernie and the Mile-Long Muffler" is an adaptation of ERNIE AND THE MILE-LONG MUFFLER by Marjorie Lewis. Text Copyright © 1982 by Marjorie Lewis. Reprinted by permission of Coward, McCann & Geoghegan.

Macmillan Publishing Company
866 Third Avenue
New York, N.Y. 10022
Collier Macmillan Canada, Inc.

Printed in the United States of America.

ISBN 0-02-163540-4

9 8 7 6 5 4 3

Contents

8

Introducing Level 9
Unit 1

Reach Out

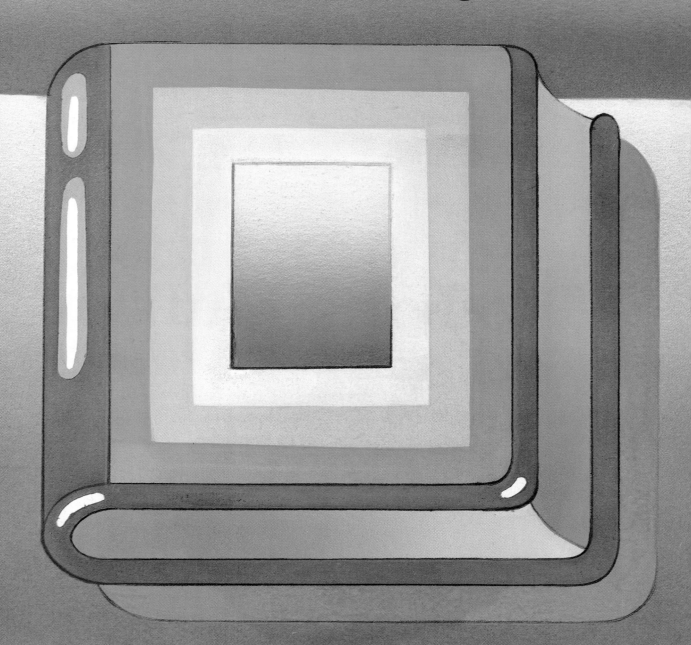

Ernie and the Mile-Long Muffler

Marjorie Lewis

Have you ever dreamed of holding a world record? Ernie, the boy in this story, tries to do just that. But what he learns along the way may be more important to him than being in a record book.

Ernie learned to knit one October afternoon when he was home waiting for the scabs from his chicken pox spots to fall off. Now that he didn't itch and feel bad, he was bored. Ernie was so bored he couldn't wait to get back to school. He wondered what exciting things his friends and Mrs. Crownfeld, his teacher, were doing while he spent his time waiting for scabs to fall off. When the doorbell suddenly rang, Ernie was glad. Even answering the door was something to do.

Ernie looked through the peephole in the door to find out who was there before opening it. He saw it was his Uncle Simon. Uncle Simon was a sailor. Ernie and his mother hadn't seen Uncle Simon in two years because he had been away at sea. Ernie had thought of Uncle Simon often during those two years. He had imagined Uncle Simon doing all the things that sailors did in the stories Ernie read.

Ernie and Uncle Simon sat and talked with each other while Ernie's mother made dinner. Uncle Simon showed Ernie pictures of the places he had been and of the ship he'd sailed on.

Uncle Simon asked Ernie what kinds of things he liked to do. Ernie told him about reading books and cereal boxes. Then he told him about trading baseball cards, making cookies, and shooting baskets.

Uncle Simon told Ernie he liked most to read mystery stories. Next, he liked to bake bread, and third, to knit. Ernie said that he didn't know that men knitted. Uncle Simon said that men have knitted for hundreds of years, especially men in armies and navies. Those men spend a lot of time waiting for things to happen.

Uncle Simon opened his seabag. He took out a sweater that looked like a rainbow. He let Ernie try it on. Ernie thought it was the most terrific sweater he had ever seen. Then Uncle Simon took some knitting needles out of his bag and a big ball of yellow yarn.

By the time Ernie's mother called them for dinner, Uncle Simon had taught Ernie to knit.

The next few days, while Ernie waited for the scabs to fall off and his spots to fade, he knitted a sweater for his dog Buster. He knitted socks for his father's golf clubs. He knitted a muffler for his mother for her birthday. The muffler was beautiful. It fit his mother's neck so well that Ernie decided to make mufflers for everyone he knew. Then he had a better idea. The idea came to him one morning while he was eating breakfast. He was reading his world-record book for the hundred millionth time. Ernie decided that he would knit the world's longest muffler. He would make it a mile long! Ernie wrote a letter to Uncle Simon, who was back at sea, and told him about his plan.

He asked his mother to get all the record books she could find in the library. Ernie looked through all of them. He found that none of them said anything about a record for muffler knitting. Ernie pictured himself holding knitting needles crossed in front of him. Foot after foot of muffler would be looped around the throne he would be sitting on when they took his picture for the record book.

Ernie told his mother about his idea. She told him that there were 5,280 feet in a mile. Then Ernie and his mother figured out that there were 63,360 inches in a mile. Ernie's mother said that it would sure be a lot of muffler to knit!

Ernie asked his mother to ask her friends to give him all the extra yarn they had. By the time Ernie was well enough to go back to school, he had finished about two feet of muffler. Ernie thought that the two feet had been done so quickly that it wouldn't be hard at all to do a mile of knitting.

His first day back at school, Ernie packed his gym bag with his gym shorts, his T-shirt, and his knitting. He kept his knitting with him all morning. He knitted when he was sitting and waiting for late-comers to be present for morning homeroom, or for the assembly program to begin. While he waited for the fire drill to be over, Ernie knitted. Mrs. Crownfeld said she thought it was wonderful to be able to knit. She asked Ernie if, after recess, he would show the class how to knit. Ernie said he would.

At recess, the class went outside. Ernie sat down on the bench to wait for his turn to shoot baskets. He took out his knitting.

"I can't believe you're doing that," said Frankie.

"I mean my *mother* does that!" said Alfred.

"So what," said Ernie. "Your mother bakes cookies, Alfred, and so do you. And so do I."

"It's different," Alfred said. "Knitting is different."

Alfred watched while Ernie's fingers made the needles form stitches. When Edward came over Frankie and Alfred moved away. Edward leaned over and watched Ernie.

"No boy I ever saw did that," Edward said. "Boys don't do that." Edward reached out and grabbed the ball of yarn, tearing it off from the knitting. Ernie watched silently while Edward, Frankie, and Alfred played basketball with the yarn ball. Then they dropped it into a puddle. They fished it out and tossed it to Ernie.

Ernie looked at the ball of yarn. It had glops of mud and leaves tangled in it. Then he put his needles and the two feet of muffler on the bench. He threw the yarn ball away into the bushes.

The three boys, Frankie, Alfred, and Edward, formed a circle around Ernie. They began to run around with their thumbs in their ears and their fingers flapping. They yelled, "Ernie knits, Ernie knits!" Over and over again. The other children in the class came over to watch. Some of them joined the group around Ernie.

By the time the bell rang for the end of recess, Ernie felt terrible. When Mrs. Crownfeld asked him to show the class how to knit, everyone began to giggle. Ernie walked up to the front of the classroom. In his hands, he held the needles and the two-foot piece of the record-making mile-long muffler. He took a deep breath and waited until the class quieted down.

He told them all about his Uncle Simon's being a sailor. He told them about the places Uncle Simon had been. He told them about Uncle Simon's terrific sweater. He told them what Uncle Simon had said about soldiers and sailors knitting while they waited for things to happen.

Finally, Ernie told the class that he was going to knit the longest muffler in the world, a mile long. He would get his name and his picture in the record books. The class was very quiet.

Mrs. Crownfeld said that she would be very proud to have one of her students set a record. Then Mrs. Crownfeld asked Ernie to show the class how to knit. Ernie said that he couldn't because he had lost his ball of yarn during recess. Ernie promised to show Mrs. Crownfeld and the class how to knit the next day.

At the end of the day, Ernie was walking home
by himself with his knitting in his gym bag.

"Ernie, Ernie," called Frankie. "Wait up!"

Frankie walked along with Ernie. "Thanks for not
telling the teacher what happened to your yarn," he
said. "I think it's neat how you're going to win the
muffler-knitting record."

Ernie and Frankie went to Ernie's house. They ate some cookies that Ernie had baked when he was sick. Ernie showed Frankie all the stuff he had knitted when he had been home with the chicken pox. Ernie next showed Frankie the bags of different-colored yarns that his mother's friends had given him for his muffler project.

"Say, Ernie," said Frankie. "I bet my mother's got some yarn left over from the sweater she knitted for my sister. I'll ask her if I can give it to you."

"That would be great, Frankie," said Ernie. "I'm going to need all the yarn I can get!"

The next day in school, Ernie showed the class how the needles went in front of the stitch to make a knit stitch. Then they went in back to make a purl stitch. He showed them how the two kinds of stitches together made the bumpy ridges that kept the sleeves tight at the wrists. He showed the class how to make the pieces get bigger and smaller to fit next to each other. Then they could be sewn together to make a swell outfit.

He offered to teach anyone in class who wanted to learn. Mrs. Crownfeld was the first to ask Ernie for lessons.

Soon everyone learned how to knit. Mrs. Crownfeld made a deal with them. The class could knit during homeroom or rainy-day recess. They could also have a special knitting time right after lunch each day. The class could knit while Mrs. Crownfeld read them a story from the library.

In return for all the knitting lessons from Ernie, the class brought in all the yarn they could get from anyone who would give it to them. Ernie kept the yarn in a big plastic garbage bag in the corner of the classroom. Each day, a knitting monitor measured Ernie's muffler and wrote the measurement in a notebook.

By Thanksgiving, Ernie's muffler was sixteen feet long. Ernie was looking pale. He never went outside to play anymore. He didn't do anything at all but go to school. At home, he would do his homework, eat, and knit. Cynthia, who was very good in math, subtracted the sixteen feet Ernie had finished from the 5,280 feet in a mile. That left 5,264 feet to go before the end of school. Since school would be over in twenty-eight weeks, Ernie would have to knit over 188 feet of muffler *every week*, or about 27 feet *every day* (including Saturday and Sunday) to finish the muffler.

Ernie listened to Cynthia very carefully. He remembered the picture he had dreamed. There he was sitting on a throne. His knitting needles would be crossed in front of him, foot after foot of muffler looping around him. His name and picture in the record books. The pride in the faces of his mother and his teacher. The admiration of all his friends. Then Ernie thought of how long it had been since he played with his friends or baked cookies or read a book—or even a cereal box.

Ernie decided to take it easy. It wasn't important when the muffler got finished. He could finish it anytime. So maybe it wouldn't be the longest muffler in the world.

Ernie told his mother, Mrs. Crownfeld, and his friends what he had decided. Now he could go out and shoot baskets during recess. He began to read his cereal boxes again. Sometimes, while he was watching television or waiting for the dentist, he would knit. If he were riding in the car, he would knit.

Ernie's class went on bringing in yarn for him. Ernie decided to give the yarn to the class. Now that they all could knit, they could have a fair to raise money to buy games and books for children in the town hospital.

All the things sold at the fair were knitted by the class. Frankie and Edward made mittens. Alfred made some bean bags. Cynthia made pot holders. Other people made mufflers (the regular length). Mrs. Crownfeld made some cat and dog sweaters. Everyone made something. The fair was a huge success. They sold $173.42 worth of stuff. That included six pairs of slipper socks in bright colors that Ernie made. It also included delicious cookies that Frankie, Alfred, and Ernie baked and sold.

By the time spring came, everyone in town knew about their knitting and Ernie's muffler. It was getting very long even if it wasn't anywhere near a mile. Then the local paper did a story about the class and took a picture to go with it. It was on the front page. Right in the middle of the photograph was Ernie, sitting on a chair, holding his knitting needles crossed in front of him. Ernie's muffler was looped around each member of the class and Mrs. Crownfeld. There were several feet to spare. It made Ernie as happy as if he had finished his mile of muffler.

Suddenly, Ernie decided the time had come. Even though people were always saying you should finish everything you start, Ernie knew better. Three hundred fourteen feet was long enough. Long enough, Ernie thought, is long enough.

He asked Mrs. Crownfeld who was an expert fringe maker to put fringe at each end of the muffler. When the muffler was done, it was exhibited all over school. People came to see it. They admired the way Ernie made all the colors of fuzzy and thin yarns come together into a multicolored muffler. People who gave yarn could see their bits. They were very pleased to see them used in Ernie's muffler.

When summer vacation came, Ernie's mother took the muffler home. Ernie helped her wrap it and put it away in a box. Then he went out to ride bikes with Frankie, Alfred, and Edward.

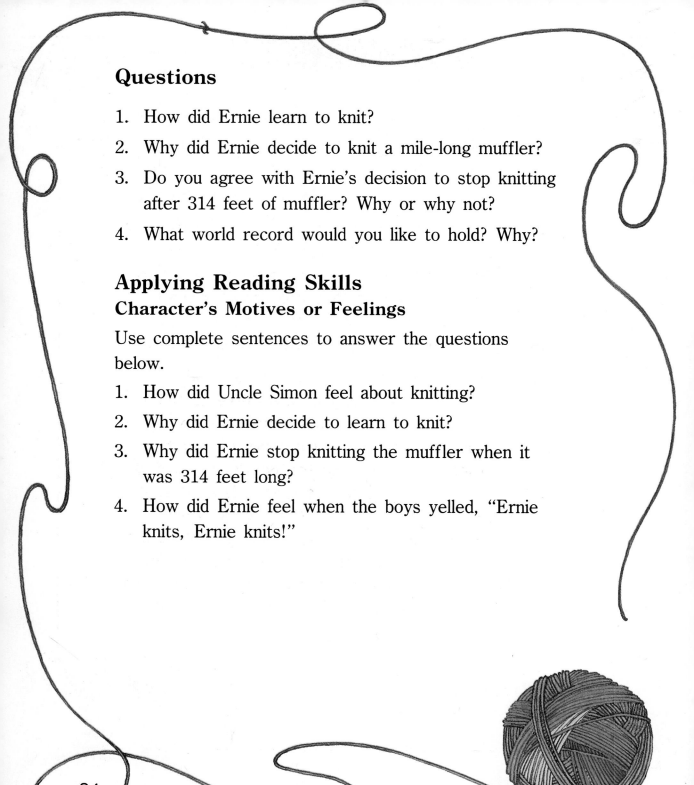

Questions

1. How did Ernie learn to knit?

2. Why did Ernie decide to knit a mile-long muffler?

3. Do you agree with Ernie's decision to stop knitting after 314 feet of muffler? Why or why not?

4. What world record would you like to hold? Why?

Applying Reading Skills
Character's Motives or Feelings

Use complete sentences to answer the questions below.

1. How did Uncle Simon feel about knitting?

2. Why did Ernie decide to learn to knit?

3. Why did Ernie stop knitting the muffler when it was 314 feet long?

4. How did Ernie feel when the boys yelled, "Ernie knits, Ernie knits!"

MILE-LONG WORDS

World-record books sometimes have information other than who knit the longest muffler or who climbed the highest mountain. Some of them also list facts like the world's tallest building or the world's longest word! Look at this word: *pneumonoultramicroscopicsilicovolcanoniosis.*

This is one of the longest words in the English language. Count how many letters make up this word! At first this word seems impossible to read, but actually there are a number of words you know inside it. Look for the words *microscopic* and *volcano* in this word. There are also parts of words that look familiar. Can you find *ultra* and *pneumono*? *Pneumono* is very close to the word *pneumonia* which is a common lung disease. And that gives you a hint about the meaning of the mile-long word. It is the name of a lung disease that some coal miners get.

Here are some long words: *incomprehensible, superconglomerate,* and *environmentalism.* Look them up in a dictionary.

25

In Which Pooh Goes Visiting and Gets Into a Tight Place

A.A. Milne
Illustrated by
Ernest H. Shepard

One of Ernie's favorite things to do was to bake cookies with his friends. In this story, the main character, a bear named Winnie-the-Pooh, just likes to eat anything with honey in it. His love for food helps to put him in a most unusual position.

Edward Bear, known to his friends as Winnie-the-Pooh, or Pooh for short, was walking through the forest one day, humming proudly to himself. He had made up a little hum that very morning, as he was doing his Stoutness Exercises in front of the glass: *Tra-la-la, tra-la-la,* as he stretched up as high as he could go, and then *Tra-la-la, tra-la—oh, help!—la,* as he tried to reach his toes.

After breakfast he had said it over and over to himself until he had learnt it off by heart, and now he was humming it right through, properly. It went like this:

Tra-la-la, tra-la-la,
Tra-la-la, tra-la-la,
Rum-tum-tiddle-um-tum.
Tiddle-iddle, tiddle-iddle,
Tiddle-iddle, tiddle-iddle,
Rum-tum-tum-tiddle-um.

Well, he was humming this hum to himself, and walking along gaily, wondering what everybody else was doing, and what it felt like, being somebody else, when suddenly he came to a sandy bank, and in the bank was a large hole.

"Aha!" said Pooh. (*Rum-tum-tiddle-um-tum.*) "If I know anything about anything, that hole means Rabbit," he said, "and Rabbit means Company," he said, "and Company means Food and Listening to Me-Humming and such like. *Rum-tum-tum-tiddle-um.*"

So he bent down, put his head into the hole, and
called out:

"Is anybody at home?"

There was a sudden scuffling noise from inside
the hole, and then silence.

"What I said was, 'Is anybody at home?'" called
out Pooh very loudly.

"No!" said a voice; and then added, "You needn't
shout so loud. I heard you quite well the first time."

"Bother!" said Pooh. "Isn't there anybody here at all?"

"Nobody."

Winnie-the-Pooh took his head out of the hole,
and thought for a little, and he thought to himself,
"There must be somebody there, because somebody
must have *said* 'Nobody.'" So he put his head back in
the hole, and said:

"Hallo, Rabbit, isn't that you?"

"No," said Rabbit, in a different sort of voice this time.

"But isn't that Rabbit's voice?"

"I don't *think* so," said Rabbit. "It isn't *meant* to be."

"Oh!" said Pooh.

He took his head out of the hole, and had
another think, and then he put it back, and said:

"Well, could you very kindly tell me where Rabbit is?"

"He has gone to see his friend Pooh Bear, who
is a great friend of his."

"But this *is* Me!" said Bear, very much surprised.

"What sort of Me?"

"Pooh Bear."

"Are you sure?" said Rabbit, still more surprised.

"Quite, quite sure," said Pooh.

"Oh, well, then, come in."

So Pooh pushed and pushed and pushed his way through the hole, and at last he got in.

"You were quite right," said Rabbit, looking at him all over. "It *is* you. Glad to see you."

"Who did you think it was?"

"Well, I wasn't sure. You know how it is in the Forest. One can't have *anybody* coming into one's house. One has to be *careful*. What about a mouthful of something?"

Pooh always liked a little something at eleven o'clock in the morning, and he was very glad to see Rabbit getting out the plates and mugs; and when Rabbit said, "Honey or condensed milk with your bread?" he was so excited that he said, "Both," and then, so as not to seem greedy, he added, "But don't bother about the bread, please." And for a long time after that he said nothing . . . until at last, humming to himself in a rather sticky voice, he got up, shook Rabbit lovingly by the paw, and said that he must be going on.

"Must you?" said Rabbit politely.

"Well," said Pooh, "I could stay a little longer if it—if you——" and he tried very hard to look in the direction of the larder.

"As a matter of fact," said Rabbit, "I was going out myself directly."

"Oh, well, then, I'll be going on. Good-bye."

"Well, good-bye, if you're sure you won't have any more."

"*Is* there any more?" asked Pooh quickly.

Rabbit took the covers off the dishes, and said, "No there wasn't."

"I thought not," said Pooh, nodding to himself. "Well, good-bye. I must be going on."

So he started to climb out of the hole. He pulled with his front paws, and pushed with his back paws, and in a little while his nose was out in the open again . . . and then his ears . . . and then his front paws . . . and then his shoulders . . . and then——

"Oh, help!" said Pooh. "I'd better go back."

"Oh, bother!" said Pooh. "I shall have to go on."

"I can't do either!" said Pooh. "Oh, help *and* bother!"

Now by this time Rabbit wanted to go for a walk too, and finding the front door full, he went out by the back door, and came round to Pooh, and looked at him.

"Hallo, are you stuck?" he asked.

"N-no," said Pooh carelessly. "Just resting and thinking and humming to myself."

"Here, give us a paw."

Pooh Bear stretched out a paw, and Rabbit pulled and pulled and pulled . . . .

"*Ow*!" cried Pooh. "You're hurting!"

"The fact is," said Rabbit, "you're stuck."

"It all comes," said Pooh crossly, "of not having front doors big enough."

"It all comes," said Rabbit sternly, "of eating too much. I thought at the time," said Rabbit, "only I didn't like to say anything," said Rabbit, "that one of us was eating too much," said Rabbit, "and I knew it wasn't *me*," he said. "Well, well, I shall go and fetch Christopher Robin."

Christopher Robin lived at the other end of the Forest, and when he came back with Rabbit, and saw the front half of Pooh, he said, "Silly old Bear," in such a loving voice that everybody felt quite hopeful again.

"I was just beginning to think," said Bear, sniffing slightly, "that Rabbit might never be able to use his front door again. And I should *hate* that," he said.

"So should I," said Rabbit.

"Use his front door again?" said Christopher Robin. "Of course he'll use his front door again."

"Good," said Rabbit.

"If we can't pull you out, Pooh, we might push you back."

Rabbit scratched his whiskers thoughtfully, and pointed out that, when once Pooh was pushed back, he was back, and of course nobody was more glad to see Pooh than *he* was, still there it was, some lived in trees and some lived underground, and—

"You mean I'd *never* get out?" said Pooh.

"I mean," said Rabbit," that having got *so* far, it seems a pity to waste it."

Christopher Robin nodded.

"Then there's only one thing to be done," he said. "We shall have to wait for you to get thin again."

"How long does getting thin take?" asked Pooh anxiously.

"About a week, I should think."

"But I can't stay here for a *week*!"

"You can *stay* here all right, silly old Bear. It's getting you out which is so difficult."

"We'll read to you," said Rabbit cheerfully. "And I hope it won't snow," he added. "And I say, old fellow, you're taking up a good deal of room in my house—*do* you mind if I use your back legs as a towel-horse? Because, I mean, there they are—doing nothing—and it would be very convenient just to hang the towels on them."

"A week!" said Pooh gloomily. "*What about meals?*"

"I'm afraid no meals," said Christopher Robin, "because of getting thin quicker. But we *will* read to you."

Bear began to sigh, and then found he couldn't because he was so tightly stuck; and a tear rolled down his eye, as he said:

"Then would you read a Sustaining Book, such as would help and comfort a Wedged Bear in Great Tightness?"

So for a week Christopher Robin read that sort of book at the North end of Pooh, and Rabbit hung his washing on the South end . . . and in between Bear felt himself getting slenderer and slenderer. And at the end of the week Christopher Robin said, *"Now!"*

So he took hold of Pooh's front paws and Rabbit took hold of Christopher Robin, and all Rabbit's friends and relations took hold of Rabbit, and they all pulled together. . . .

And for a long time Pooh only said *"Ow!"*

And then all of a sudden, he said *"Pop!"* just as if a cork were coming out of a bottle.

And Christopher Robin and Rabbit and all Rabbit's friends and relations went head-over-heels backwards . . . and on the top of them came Winnie-the-Pooh—free!

So, with a nod of thanks to his friends, he went on with his walk through the forest, humming proudly to himself. But, Christopher Robin looked after him lovingly, and said to himself, "Silly old Bear!"

Questions

1. What was Winnie-the-Pooh doing in front of the glass?

2. How did Pooh get caught in Rabbit's hole?

3. Why do you think Pooh wanted to visit Rabbit?

4. What are some other ways you could have helped Pooh get out of his tight place?

Applying Reading Skills
Best Title for a Story

Look back at "In Which Pooh Goes Visiting and Gets Into a Tight Place." Write a sentence that tells why this was a good title for the story. Now look at these titles for the same story. Which one do you like best and why?

a. Run-tum-tiddle-um-tum
b. Rabbit and Pooh
c. A Wedged Bear

SKILLS
activity

SKILLS ACTIVITY
GRAPHIC AIDS: MAPS

When you need to find the way to go somewhere, you can use a map. Maps show where things are. A map key shows what things on a map stand for. Using the key on a map can help you find a place you are looking for.

Knowing directions helps you find places more easily, too. North is the direction toward the North Pole. When you face north, east is to your right. West is to your left, and south is behind you. North, east, south, and west are four main directions. They are known as **cardinal directions.**

A compass helps you find directions. When a compass is held flat, its needle points north. A compass rose can help you find directions on a map. A compass rose is a circle design showing directions. Find the compass rose on the map. How are north, south, east, and west marked?

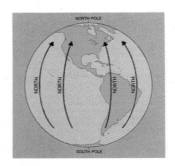

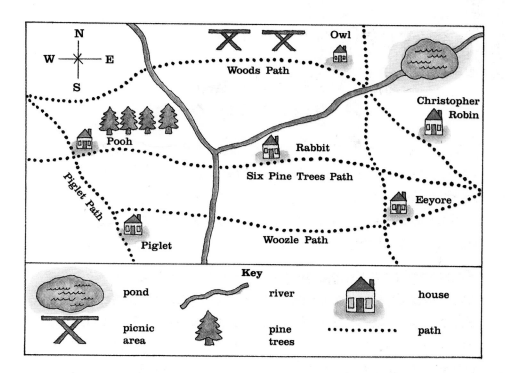

Looked at the map. It shows where Winnie-the-Pooh and his friends live in the forest. Study the key and compass rose. Answer the questions on your paper.

1. What does 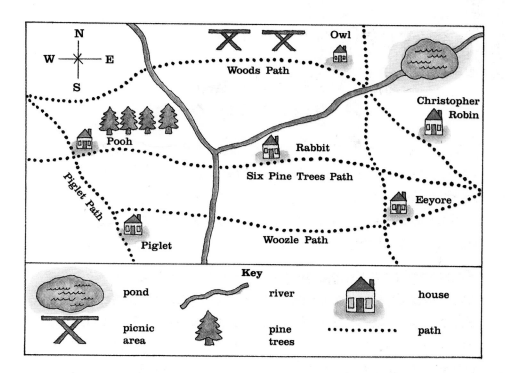 stand for on the map?

2. In what direction would Pooh travel to go from his house to Christopher Robin's house?

3. What area is north of Woods Path?

4. What path would Piglet take to go from his house to Eeyore's house? In what direction would he travel?

5. Christopher Robin and Pooh want to meet at someone's house. Whose house is about halfway between them?

6. What is east of Owl's house and north of Christopher Robin's house?

KATY DID IT

Victoria Boutis

Winnie-the-Pooh got into a tight place, and his friends, Christopher Robin and Rabbit, faced the challenge of getting him out. Katy, the girl in this story, has some problems when she decides to join her father and her dog Toby on a three-day hike in the Adirondack Mountains.

The hike went along fine at first. Katy learned to read the trail markings and she skipped along the trail easily. Then things took a turn for the worse.

The trail became steeper and more rocky. For the first time, Katy knew that she was climbing. Her breath came in short, loud pants. Her heart banged against her chest. A muscle in the back of her leg began to hurt. Her pack felt heavy on her back.

"Ohhh," Katy groaned. "How much farther?"

"Just another half mile. Let's hurry," Mr. Milonas said. "I think it's starting to rain."

Mr. Milonas helped Katy get out the red poncho he had told her to pack "just in case." The hood of the poncho came out over her head. It was made to keep rain out, but it didn't work. A thin stream of water fell onto Katy's nose.

"This isn't any fun," Katy said. She lagged behind her father.

The rain had dampened Toby's spirits, too. He walked beside Katy now, stopping every few minutes to shake the water from his coat.

"That wasn't so bad, was it?" Mr. Milonas asked Katy when she finally dragged her wet self up to the flat place he had chosen for their first night's camp. Through the rain Katy could hear him whistling "Oh, what a beautiful morning . . ."

"It's not beautiful and it's not morning," Katy grumped. Her feet hurt. Her shoulders were sore, and she was hungry. "What time is supper?" she asked.

Mr. Milonas looked at Katy. "This restaurant, Madame, serves dinner at six-thirty," he said, bowing low. "Or whenever the cook comes."

In spite of her bad mood, Katy laughed. Her father acted so silly sometimes. Of course Katy knew that she would just have to wait until her father finished setting up the tarps and tents, rolling out the mats and shaking out the sleeping bags. Unless . . . Katy's stomach growled. "Can I make supper?" Katy asked.

"That would be great," Mr. Milonas said. "I'll light the stove for you."

Now that she had something to do, Katy felt much better. "I think," she said, "we'll have the beef stew."

"Call me when supper's ready," Mr. Milonas said.

Katy read the directions on the package:

DIRECTIONS
ADD CONTENTS OF PACKAGE TO 2 CUPS BOILING WATER.

COOK 5 MINUTES
STIR OCCASIONALLY
SERVES FOUR

She took a pot from her pack. She opened one of the canteens and poured water to the 2-cup mark. She set the pot on the stove and covered it. "That was easy," she said. "Now I'll set the table."

Katy listened to the rain on the tarp. It was a cheery sound, reminding her that she was dry under it. She stirred the stew. It was thick and bubbly. She called, "Supper's ready."

But the sound of the rain blotted out her words. She gave the stew a final stir. Then she ducked out from under the cover of the tarp. She dashed over to where her father was tapping a tent peg into the ground. "Supper's ready," she repeated. "Come on."

"Great!" Mr. Milonas said. "I could eat a horse."

They hurried back toward the tarp just as it fell at one end. A wall of water surged past their faces.

Katy ran over to the pot and looked in. Water, as well as dirt, leaves, and twigs covered the stew. "Oh no!" she wailed. "It's ruined!"

Mr. Milonas came up behind her and looked into the pot. "Don't worry," he said. "We'll have soup instead of stew." He poured some into each cup, skimmed off the top layer of leaves and began to eat.

"I'm not eating this," Katy said.

But Mr. Milonas said, "When you go camping, you have to make the best of what you have."

"Make the best!" Katy tossed the words back. "I did make the best. I set the table. I made supper. It's your fault. Your tarp fell down."

43

"Hey, Katy-did. I'm sorry," Mr. Milonas said. He put an arm around her shoulder and said reasonably, "It's only a little water. How about some oatmeal bread?"

But Katy didn't want to be reasonable. "No," she said. "I'm not hungry now. Want some stew, Toby?" she asked, and put her supper in his bowl.

"Tomorrow will be better," Mr. Milonas said. "Today wasn't so bad. I can still picture you leaping across those streams like a mountain goat."

Katy didn't answer.

"I think the cure for your problem is a good night's sleep," Mr. Milonas said. "C'mon, I'll tuck you in."

Though she was still angry, Katy let herself be led to her tent. Mr. Milonas helped her unlace her boots. She climbed into the clammy sleeping bag.

"Don't you want to get undressed?" her father asked.

"No," Katy said. She shivered inside the sleeping bag. "I'm too cold."

"All right, then. I'll be right here if you need me." He kissed her. "Good night," he said.

Katy curled up inside the bag and closed her eyes. But she couldn't sleep. She thought about the different foods she would like to be eating now. Blueberry muffins spread with sweet butter. Cinnamon toast and cocoa. Warm, homey foods. The kind her mother made on dreary days or when Katy stayed home from school with a cold. Yes. That was what she needed now. Someone to fix her a warming snack, to take care of her.

Katy shut her eyes, but she was wide awake, and there were strange noises around her. She heard rustles and scratches, as though a furry animal were running over the tent. "Daddy," she called. "Are you up?"

"What . . . ?"

"What's that noise? There's something on my tent."

"It's just a branch scraping against the side."

"Daddy?"

"Yes?"

"It's very dark in here."

"Why don't you turn on your flashlight for a while?"

Katy fished her stubby flashlight from the pocket of her pack and turned it on. Yes. That was better. After a while Katy turned off the flashlight. Toby sighed. Katy was asleep.

Katy woke to the sounds of breakfast pots banging and Toby crying to be let out. Then she remembered. "I slept out all night." She smiled at the thought.

"Well, good morning," Mr. Milonas said.

"It's freezing," Katy answered, blowing out breath that was a white puff in the air.

"Brisk," her father said cheerily, his breath also a puff of white. "A lovely, brisk morning." He handed Katy her Sierra cup. It was filled with oatmeal and smelled delicious. Sweet and cinnamony.

Katy ate quickly. With the oatmeal warming her insides, she had to admit that it wasn't freezing after all. Just brisk.

"Ready to go?" Mr. Milonas said.

"Uh huh," Katy nodded. But she waited. She looked at the small clearing that had been home for a night. There were no clues that two people and a dog had been there.

Katy looked up at the huge tree above her. She thought of the hikers' motto that she had seen posted at the entrance of many trails. "Take nothing but pictures. Leave nothing but footprints." That was the way it should be, she knew. But even the muddy footprints they left would be covered with fallen leaves or washed away with the next rain.

She waved a quiet good-bye to the campsite and turned away.

"Did you see that?" Mr. Milonas stopped suddenly. "A weasel just crossed the trail, right in front of me. It had a mouse in its mouth."

Katy stared into the bushes. The weasel was gone.

Katy fixed her eyes on her feet. She didn't want to look at her boots, where dried mud was flaking off at the tip. But she had to watch where she put each foot. The trail was narrow and turning here. There were sharp rocks just waiting to trip her. There were wet moss-covered patches.

"It's not fair," she said. "You see everything first."

"Keep looking," her father answered. "I'm sure you'll see something interesting." They went on walking.

"How about some gorp?" Mr. Milonas asked, handing Katy a fat plastic bag.

Katy couldn't pass up gorp. "Yummm," she said, taking a handful into her mouth. Someone had told her that gorp was short for Good Old Raisins and Peanuts. But the gorp her father put together was always more interesting than that. Today's gorp was a mixture of chopped dates, granola, dried apples, and butterscotch bits. Of course, it had raisins and peanuts.

Mr. Milonas had stopped to talk with another hiker. There was a hikers' code that Katy knew. They always stopped to talk on the trail. Even though they didn't know each other, just being hikers made them part of a club. It was as though Katy were part of that club when she said, "Beautiful day, isn't it?"

"Oh," the hiker shrugged, "I've climbed thirty-seven mountains in the past ten days. One day is just like another to me." He gave Katy a small smile, nodded to her father, and edged past them.

"I wonder why he bothers then," Katy said. She noticed for the first time since early that morning that it was, in fact, a beautiful day. The few cottony clouds made the blue sky even bluer. The sun was bright— almost hot. But there was a gentle breeze that cooled her head.

Katy raised her eyes from the rocky trail. The forest was lovely. Here the trees were slender and young looking. She looked up at the leafy branch above her. The air seemed perfectly still just then. But, as she watched, one leaf detached itself and fell to her boot top. It was deep green with a thin edge of red. It was as though someone had outlined it with a pen. Katy's first leaf of fall. She picked it up. Then she ran to catch up with her father.

"Daddy," she called. "Look what I found!"

Questions

1. How did Katy feel when she and her father reached the area where they would camp?

2. Why is "Take nothing but pictures. Leave nothing but footprints" the hikers' motto?

3. Do you think Katy will go hiking again? Why or why not?

4. If you had the chance to go hiking, what would you take with you?

Applying Reading Skills
Character's Motives or Feelings

Use complete sentences to answer the questions below.

1. How did Katy feel when her father whistled "Oh, what a beautiful morning . . ."?

2. Why did Katy laugh when her father pretended to be the owner of a restaurant?

3. Why did Mr. Milonas tell Katy not to worry about the stew being covered by water, dirt, leaves, and twigs?

4. Why do you think the hiker on the trail said that one day was like another to him?

When I Am Me

I'm impossible . . . possible,
breaking away from the
hard-holding hand
and flinging myself
in the air
on the sea
on a wave in the land.
And thrashing about
just impossibly . . . possibly,
calling—no, yelling—
as loud as I can,
I am me!
I am me!
I can do anything.
I can run
to the end of the land
if I want to
or swim to the end of the sea
if I want to.
      I want to—not now,
      but I want to
      and will when it's possible . . .
      really is possible.
      Everything's possible
      when I am me.

Felice Holman

Lorenzo & Angelina

Eugene Fern

Katy came to appreciate the beauty
of the mountains. Angelina Garcia,
the girl in this story, is eager to see
the world from the top of El Padre
Mountain. Her donkey, Lorenzo, has
his own opinion.

54

 Angelina's story

Every morning, when the air is fresh and the dew lies like shining jewels over the fields and trees, I go to Lorenzo's stable. I carry with me the milk which Umberto has put into a heavy wooden barrel and the eggs which Jacinta has carefully packed in a wooden box. I open the door and out comes Lorenzo. "Good morning, my Lorenzo," I say. I pat his back, rub the top of his head, and give him a hug. Then I pack the barrel and box on him and I am ready to leave for the village.

But not Lorenzo!

 Lorenzo's story

Every morning, when Angelina comes to let me out of my house, she is glad to see me. She rubs my head, puts her face next to mine, gives me a squeeze, and says, "Good morning, my Lorenzo."

And every morning, to be sure, I am glad to see her too—that is, until she starts to scold.

Angelina's story

Every morning it is the same. I talk to him politely, but he looks this way and that. He smells the air. He chews the grass. He nibbles at the clover. He does everything but what he is supposed to do!

I begin to lose my temper, of course. I shout at him. He pays no attention. He stands like a rock.

Though I love him dearly, there is no doubt that my Lorenzo is the most stubborn creature in the whole world.

Lorenzo's story

Every morning, Angelina says, "Lorenzo, it is time for us to go to the village, so please begin to walk." But anyone should know I am not yet ready to go. I have to smell the morning air. I have to chew the grass under the eucalyptus tree.

"Lorenzo," she says, "let us go this very minute." But I am still too busy. "Move, you stubborn donkey!" she screams. "Move those stubborn feet!"

But of course I have to see if the house is in the right place, if the south fence has moved, if the sheep are where they're supposed to be. Naturally, I cannot leave yet.

It is only when she stamps her feet that I move. I am very fond of Angelina and don't like to see her upset, but is it not wrong for her to insult me this way?

 Angelina's story

One morning, like all the other times, we finally set out for the village. My stubborn Lorenzo had finished whatever it was he was doing, and I could tell by the way his ears stood straight up and by the quick movements of his feet that he was as pleased as I to leave for the marketplace at Cuzoroca.

 ## Lorenzo's story

One morning we finally set out for the village. Angelina had finished shouting and stamping. As always, she was happy once we started. I could tell by the way she began to sing and laugh—and every once in a while to skip along the road. She liked the little trip to the village, and, to tell the truth, so did I.

Angelina's story

However, this day was to be different, for I had decided to go to the top of El Padre Mountain! Ever since I can remember, I had heard of the beauty and the glory to be seen from there. It is said that from the top of El Padre one can touch the sky.

I was so excited about my great adventure that I hardly knew where I was going.

Lorenzo's story

This day was like all other days. We went beside El Padre Mountain, through Quesada Pass, across the flat meadows, through the forest, and into the village.

Angelina's story

When we came to the marketplace, I quickly took care of my business with Señor Vives. He counted the eggs, weighed the milk, and paid me for them. I thanked him politely and then I climbed on Lorenzo's back. I could hardly wait to begin the trip to the top of El Padre Mountain!

As one might expect, when we came to the crossroads my stubborn donkey refused to move. Only after much shouting did he agree to take the right fork instead of the left.

 **Lorenzo's story**

Señor Vives was at his place, as usual. He took the milk and eggs from my back, counted the eggs, weighed the milk, and paid Angelina for them. As usual, he took the money from his strong little box under the counter. Then, as usual, we started for home.

But things no longer went as usual, for Angelina decided to go home a different way. Instead of taking the left turn after the road leaves the forest, she decided to take the right. At first I wouldn't budge. Who knows what might be in a strange land? Finally, with all her shouting, I gave in and went where *she* wanted to go!

Angelina's story

This road was different from the hard dirt road leading to our farm. It passed over rushing streams, between tall trees and huge rocks, always moving up—higher and higher. It was rough and rocky, and the higher we went, the rougher it got. Though I knew the sun would soon be sinking, I was determined to reach the top of El Padre Mountain. Lorenzo moved more and more slowly, but I urged him on.

Soon the road had almost disappeared. There was nothing ahead of us but a little rocky path. It was getting dark and Lorenzo stopped. Again I had to shout and scold until he moved on.

 ## Lorenzo's story

This road was not like the other. It was rough and rocky. It did not go through Quesada Pass but behind it, toward the top of El Padre Mountain. Higher and higher we climbed, and the higher we went, the harder it was to see the road. Soon there was no road at all, just a rocky path.

And still Angelina had to explore!

Once or twice I stopped, but she shouted so much that I kept moving. It was growing dark, and we were up so high I could hardly breathe. There were rocks on all sides, and every once in a while a poor little bush.

 ## Angelina's story

Though the wind was stronger and the path even rockier than before, I was not worried. My Lorenzo is as sure-footed as a mountain goat and I knew he would not fall. Besides, any moment I expected to see the glory and beauty of our country, and this would make everything worthwhile.

But once more my stubborn donkey refused to go. Again I had to scream to make him move those stubborn legs.

 ## Lorenzo's story

I was getting worried. It was not easy to walk, and I knew that if I stumbled we would have a long fall before we reached the good earth again.

So once more I stopped, but my little Angelina insisted on climbing that mountain. She shouted. "Stubborn, stubborn donkey!" she screamed at me.

So what was there to do but move higher and still higher?

 ## Angelina's story

It was when we came to two huge rocks that stood like sentinels over the others that Lorenzo made up his mind not to move another inch. He sat down in front of the rocks in such a way that not even a tiny lizard could pass by.

 ## Lorenzo's story

Finally, what seemed to be the path went between two huge rocks. And then it ended! A bush grew between the rocks, and after that— who knows?

This time I decided the trip was over. Not another step would I take!

I sat down.

 ## Angelina's story

I yelled at Lorenzo. I shouted. I pleaded. I screamed. I pulled at him. I pushed him from behind. He would not budge. He sat there looking like one more rock, among all the others.

 ## Lorenzo's story

The great explorer Angelina did not take to this kindly. Her shouts before were as nothing compared to the noise she now made. "Move!" she screamed. "We are almost at the top!" She pushed and pulled me. Tears of anger were in her eyes, but it did no good. This time I would not take another step.

 ## Angelina's story

At this very moment I heard footsteps, and there behind us appeared my father, followed by Señor Vives and Señor Quiñones of the police. Suddenly I realized how late it must be. I was sure Papá would be furious. Instead he picked me up and kissed me. All he said was:

"Little one, I am not angry because you took the right turn instead of the left. Children are always looking for new paths. This I understand. But why have you stayed so long? Didn't you know your mother and I would be worried? Everyone is looking for you."

I tried to explain how much I wanted to see the glory of the world from the top of El Padre Mountain and how much time I had wasted trying to get that stubborn Lorenzo to move.

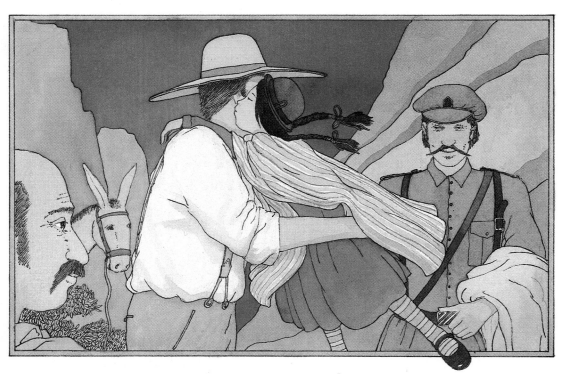

 Lorenzo's story

Suddenly there were sounds behind us and who should appear but Señor Garcia, Señor Vives, and Señor Quiñones of the police! How happy they were to see us! Señor Garcia picked up little Angelina. He hugged her and whispered to her, while the other gentlemen, with big smiles, slapped him on the back.

Angelina looked ashamed and said, "I did so much want to see the top of the mountain, Papá, but that stubborn Lorenzo would not move. He simply refused to budge."

 Angelina's story

Papá said nothing. He took my hand and led me between the two huge rocks. He pushed the little bush aside so I could see beyond it. I looked and my knees turned to water! Beyond the bush was the end of the path and also the end of the mountain. Had Lorenzo and I taken but one step beyond the bush, we should never have taken a step again!

 Lorenzo's story

Señor Garcia did not say a word. He took Angelina by the hand and led her between the two rocks. Beyond the bush was nothing—no path, no rocks, just nothing.

It was, of course, as *I* suspected. What could one expect to find up here so near the sky, where even the poorest bush finds it difficult to breathe?

Angelina said nothing. She just stood there, pale and trembling. My poor Angelina!

 ## Angelina's story

I do not remember too clearly what happened after that, for I was weak from fear and could hardly stand. But I do remember one thing. Seeing that dear, stubborn donkey standing there, I felt such a love for him that I kissed him gently and whispered, "Thank you, my Lorenzo!"

 ## Lorenzo's story

Señor Garcia said, "You should be grateful to have such a stubborn donkey, my little flower. If not for him, I would have neither Angelina nor Lorenzo." He put his arms around my neck and gave me such a squeeze that I could hardly breathe. When Angelina kissed me, my happiness was complete.

68

Questions

1. What does Angelina take to the village every morning?

2. What did Angelina and Lorenzo disagree about?

3. Do you think Angelina will continue to shout at Lorenzo and stamp her feet when he is stubborn?

4. When would being stubborn about something be useful? When would it not?

Applying Reading Skills
Facts and Opinions

"Lorenzo and Angelina" is about two different opinions or ways of viewing things. Write these headings on your paper:

    Lorenzo's Opinions   Angelina's Opinions

Write each sentence below under the correct heading.

1. Lorenzo does everything but what he is supposed to.

2. Lorenzo has many things to check on before he can go to the village.

3. The top of El Padre Mountain must be the most beautiful place on earth.

4. The poorest bush finds it difficult to breathe so near the sky.

5. Lorenzo is the most stubborn creature in the whole world.

SKILLS activity

FACTS AND OPINIONS

Statements that can be proved true or false are called **facts.** Sentences that tell what someone thinks or feels about something are called **opinions.**

Look at the picture. Read the sentence below the picture.

The donkey is in the barn.

This sentence is a **fact.** It is true. You can prove it because you can see that there is a donkey in the barn.

Now read this sentence.

Donkeys are the most stubborn creatures in the whole world.

This sentence is an **opinion.** You cannot prove it. It is what someone thinks or believes about donkeys.

The difference between a fact and an opinion is that a fact *can* be proven. An opinion cannot be proven.

ACTIVITY A Read each pair of sentences. On your paper write the sentence that is a fact.

1. We need food to live.
   Pooh thinks honey is the best food.
2. A friend can help you out of a tight spot.
   A friend is someone you like.
3. Tea and honey cakes are delicious.
   A honeybee makes and stores honey.
4. Pooh did Stoutness Exercises.
   Exercises can be fun.

ACTIVITY B Read each pair of sentences. On your paper write the sentence that is an opinion.

5. Cereal boxes are interesting to read.
   Some books have pictures in them.
6. Books have been written about world records.
   It's easy to hold a world record.
7. Donkeys make great pets.
   Donkeys can be used to carry things.
8. Some people have climbed very high mountains.
   Animals shouldn't climb mountains.

71

A Box Full Of Infinity

Jay Williams

In this play, Ben—a poor prince—sets out to seek his fortune. Along the way, he helps an old woman who, in return, gives him a mysterious box. Find out how the "box full of Infinity" helps Ben reach his goal.

The Players		
Poor King	Rich King	Pretzel
Ben	Wizard	Storyteller
Old Woman	Princess	

Storyteller: Once there was a king who was very poor. He had one castle, one servant, one soldier, and one cow. He also had one son named Ben. One day the Poor King was talking to his son.

Poor King: Ben, my boy, I have given you all I can. You know how to work and how to enjoy yourself. You know how to read and write and how to count up to ten thousand. I have nothing more to give you except some advice. My advice is this: Set out and seek your fortune.

Ben: Very well, Father. When I have found it, I will give you some.

Storyteller: Ben started walking briskly down the road, whistling as he walked. Soon he sat down to rest. He had just begun to eat when he saw an old woman.

Old Woman: *(crying)* Oh, dear, I am so hungry! I want some soup, but I cannot lift down my big iron pot from this high tree.

Ben: I'll lift it down for you.

Old Woman: Thank you, but now I must have some water for my soup.

Ben: *(going to the stream and filling the pot)* I'll get you some water.

Old Woman: That's fine, but the water must be hot.

Ben: *(cutting some wood)* I'll build you a fire so that you can put the pot over it.

Old Woman: But now I must have something to make soup with. A piece of meat would be nice.

Storyteller: Ben sighed and gave his meat to the Old Woman.

Old Woman: Fine, but soup is no good without bread.

Storyteller: Again Ben sighed and gave her his loaf of bread.

Ben: *(talking to himself)* Well, well. I have been poor all my life. I don't mind having nothing.

Old Woman: You must be hungry after doing all that work. Sit down now and eat some dinner.

Storyteller: They both had dinner.

Old Woman: You are a good young man. You are not afraid of work, and you have a kind heart. I must do something for you.

Storyteller: She took out a little box and opened it. Inside, there was a golden pretzel, which she gave to Ben.

Ben: How can I eat a golden pretzel?

Old Woman: You do not eat it. Keep it in the box. It is called *Infinity*. It is the most of anything there is. It goes on forever and has no end.

Ben: I see. What good is it?

Old Woman: I don't know, but some day you may be able to use it. However, you can only use it once. So think well before you do so.

Ben: *(putting it in his pocket)* Thank you.

Storyteller: Next day Ben came to a splendid city, but all the people were very sad and wore black. Ben went to the castle to see the king.

Rich King: My daughter has been stolen away by a wizard and no one knows how to get her back. I will give a fortune to the man who saves her.

Ben: Fine! I am looking for my fortune. I will try.

Storyteller: Ben went to find the wizard.

Ben: *(going up to the wizard)* I'm looking for a job.

Wizard: What can you do?

Ben: I can dig better than that girl.

Storyteller: Ben pointed to the girl in the garden who was digging. She had a crown on her head.

Wizard: Very well, I'll hire you.

Ben: What will you pay me?

Wizard: If you work for me for thirty days and a day, and do everything I say, I will answer any question you ask.

Storyteller: So Ben did many jobs for the wizard and became friends with the sad princess. At the end of the thirty days and a day, Ben went back to the wizard.

Ben: Now you must answer my question. How can I set the princess free?

Wizard: *(laughing a nasty laugh)* It will do you no good to know. You must beat me in three contests. That is the only way to set the princess free.

Ben: It doesn't sound easy, but I think I'll try.

Wizard: All right. The first contest is a race. We will start from the house and run to that tree. The first one there wins.

Ben: *(talking to himself)* I wonder if I ought to use the golden pretzel? Maybe it would make me run faster than anything. But then I can only use it once, and if I win this race I still have two more contests. Perhaps I had better think hard instead.

Ben: *(talking to the wizard)* Since your legs are longer than mine, I ought to have a head start.

Wizard: Very well, go halfway there. *(Ben goes halfway.)*

Wizard: I will count to three. One . . . two . . .

Ben: Just a minute! You have already lost the race.

Wizard: What? How have I lost? We haven't even started to run.

Ben: Well, first you have to run from where you are to where I am. Right?

Wizard: Of course.

Ben: But before you run that distance, you have to run half of it.

Wizard: But—

Ben: And before you can run that half, you have to run half of it. And before you can run that half, you have to run half of that.

Wizard: So?

Ben: So I don't think you can move at all.

Storyteller: The wizard scratched his head trying to figure it out. While he was trying, Ben ran quickly to the tree.

Ben: You see? I was right. You lost.

Storyteller: The wizard scowled.

Ben: What's next?

79

Wizard: The second contest is to see who can make the loudest noise.

Ben: *(to himself)* Maybe now I ought to use the golden pretzel. Perhaps it would make me shout louder than anything. No. I can only use it once and there is still another contest after this. I'd better think hard instead.

Ben: *(to the wizard)* You begin, since you're older than I am.

Storyteller: The wizard yelled as loud as he could. It was a terrible noise. Stones bounced. Houses trembled.

Wizard: There, beat that if you can!

Storyteller: Ben took out a pin and jabbed it into the wizard's leg. The wizard yelled. The ground shook. Rocks split in two. It was a louder sound than before.

Ben: I won.

Wizard: *(jumping up and down in anger)* How did you win? *I* was the one who yelled.

Ben: That's true, but the contest was to see who could make the loudest noise. I made you yell. So I made the noise.

Wizard: Trickery!

Storyteller: The wizard was so angry that the air around him turned green. Then he became very calm.

Wizard: Very well, but you must beat me in the third contest, and this time no trick will help you. The last contest is to see who can count the highest.

Storyteller: Ben grew pale. Although he knew how to do many things, he could only count up to ten thousand.

Ben: *(to himself)* Now I must use my box full of Infinity.

Storyteller: Ben took out the golden pretzel.

Wizard: *(counting as fast as he can)* . . . one million!

Pretzel: *(in a voice like Ben's)* And one more.

and one more...

81

Wizard: *(counting fast again)* . . . one trillion!

Pretzel: And one more.

Storyteller: The wizard continued counting. Ben ran and got the princess. They rode away on his horse to the splendid city and back to the Rich King, who now was a happy king. Ben married the princess and took her home to his own castle. He gave his father, the Poor King, half the fortune so that he became a rich king. As for the wizard, he is still counting. He will count forever. No matter how high he counts, the pretzel will always say . . .

Pretzel: And one more.

Questions

1. What advice did Ben's father give him?
2. Why did a golden pretzel stand for *Infinity*?
3. Do you think Ben won the first two contests fair and square?
4. If Ben didn't have the golden pretzel, how might he have won the last contest?

Applying Reading Skills
Draw Conclusions

Read each conclusion below. Then write two or three sentences that give information to support the conclusion.

1. The girl who was digging in the wizard's garden was the princess.
2. The wizard could count higher than Ben.
3. Ben received the golden pretzel because he was a kind person.
4. Ben knew exactly when to use the golden pretzel.

BEHIND THE SCENES OF A BROADWAY MUSICAL

BY BILL POWERS

What is it like to be in a play? This photo-essay takes you "behind the scenes"—from rehearsals to previews to opening night. You will meet a group of young actors preparing for a Broadway musical. The photographs will help show you what is involved in getting ready for a production.

Nine young actors were lined up on the stage. Their faces were stretched in smiles. Their top hats waved in the air. The opening night audience in the packed theater smiled back. They were clapping in time to the music. The cast bowed. The audience clapped on and on. The first performance of Maurice Sendak's *Really Rosie* was over. After all the hard work it seemed like a magic time. The cast stood straight again. They looked at each other and smiled. Then they bowed again.

Five weeks earlier, the scenery behind the actors had not been made. Neither had the costumes they wore nor the top hats they were waving above their heads. Five weeks earlier, the stage they were standing on was an empty space.

Really Rosie tells the story of how some kids on a Brooklyn street spend a hot, boring summer day. With nothing to do, they look to Rosie to entertain them. Rosie has a dream of becoming a movie star. She makes up the story for a movie about her rise to stardom—and her search for her lost brother, Chicken Soup. (Chicken Soup is really not lost, but hiding in a large cardboard box.) All the kids try out for her movie. Rosie tells the story of Chicken Soup's disappearance. At the end of the play, Rosie rewards them all with parts in the "movie of her life."

The casting of *Really Rosie* took a long time. Director Pat Birch auditioned more than 150 children. There were six main characters in the play and one smaller part, the Lion.

After many long hours, the parts were filled. Birch felt that the actors she picked would bring a special feeling to the play. They would bring life to Sendak's characters.

Rosie would be played by Tisha Campbell (age 11) and Kathy, by April Lerman (11). Pierre would be played by B. J. Barie (8) and Johnny, by Wade Raley (8). Joey LaBenz IV (7) would play Alligator and Jermaine Campbell (7) would be Chicken Soup. Matthew Kolmes would be the Lion. Ruben Cuevas and Lara Berk would fill in for the other actors whenever necessary.

Rehearsals begin. Director Pat Birch asks the cast to think about their characters.

Pat and Tisha (Rosie) work on the opening speech in the play. Behind them, stagehands get the scenery ready.

The cast rehearses "Pierre." It is one of the longest and hardest musical numbers in the show.

Musical director Joel Silberman works with the cast on a song.

The cast tries on their costumes for dress rehearsal. Because Tisha was so active on stage, the brim of her hat had to be pinned back.

When B.J. wore his T-shirt for the first time, it looked too clean. A few days later, it looked more in character.

In his Alligator hat and green overalls, Joey waits on stage to be checked.

Even curtain calls have to be practiced. Pat leads the cast in a rehearsal of the curtain call.

Previews are performances that test a play in front of a paying audience.

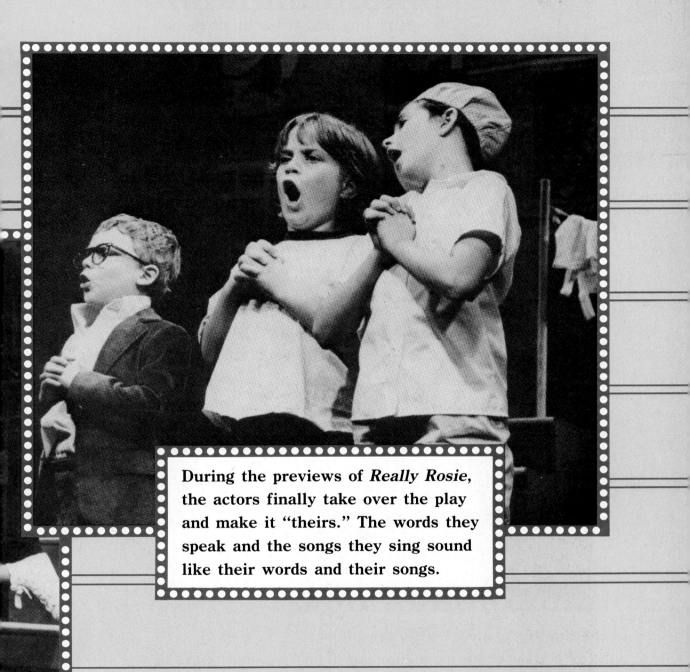

During the previews of *Really Rosie*, the actors finally take over the play and make it "theirs." The words they speak and the songs they sing sound like their words and their songs.

It is Opening Night! In the dressing room, a wardrobe person helps Joey with his costume.

In the lighting control booth, the lighting person waits for a cue from the stage manager before the play begins.

Backstage, stagehands get ready to raise the curtain.

A golden light covers Tisha as she stands in the center of the stage. She spreads her arms and begins to sing. "I'm really Rosie . . ."

And she really is.

Questions

1. How long did it take from the time the production began until opening night?
2. Why did the casting of *Really Rosie* take so long?
3. How do you think the actors felt opening night?
4. If you were involved in a play, would you want to be an actor or one of the members of the crew? Explain why.

Applying Reading Skills
Best Title for a Story

Look back at "Behind the Scenes of a Broadway Musical." Write a sentence that tells why this was a good title for the story. Now look at these titles for the same story. Which one do you like best and why?

a. Really Rosie Really Happens!
b. And the Audience Clapped On
c. A Magic Time

PIERRE

MAURICE SENDAK

PROLOGUE

There once was a boy named Pierre
who only would say,
"I don't care!"
Read his story, my friend,
for you'll find at the end
that a suitable moral lies there.

CHAPTER 1

One day his mother said
when Pierre climbed out of bed,
"Good morning, darling boy,
you are my only joy."
Pierre said, *"I don't care!"*
"What would you like to eat?"
"I don't care!"
"Some lovely cream of wheat?"
"I don't care!"
"Don't sit backwards on your chair."
"I don't care!"
"Or pour syrup on your hair."
"I don't care!"
"You are acting like a clown."
"I don't care!"
"And we have to go to town."
"I don't care!"

"Don't you want to come, my dear?"
"I don't care!"
"Would you rather stay right here?"
"I don't care!"
So his mother left him there.

CHAPTER 2

His father said, "Get off your head
or I will march you up to bed!"
Pierre said, *"I don't care!"*
"I would think that you could see—"
"I don't care!"
"Your head is where
your feet should be!"
"I don't care!"
"If you keep standing upside down—"
"I don't care!"
"We'll never ever get to town."
"I don't care!"
"If only you would say I CARE."
"I don't care!"
"I'd let you fold the folding chair."
"I don't care!"
So his parents left him there.
They didn't take him anywhere.

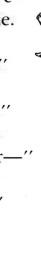

CHAPTER 3

Now, as the night began to fall
a hungry lion paid a call.
He looked Pierre right in the eye
and asked him if he'd like to die.
Pierre said, *"I don't care!"*
"I can eat you, don't you see?"
"I don't care!"
"And you will be inside of me."
"I don't care!"
"Then you'll never have to bother—"
"I don't care!"
"With a mother and a father."
"I don't care!"
"Is that all you have to say?"
"I don't care!"
"Then I'll eat you, if I may."
"I don't care!"
So the lion ate Pierre.

CHAPTER 4

Arriving home at six o'clock,
his parents had a dreadful shock!
They found the lion sick in bed
and cried, "Pierre is surely dead!"
They pulled the lion by the hair.
They hit him with the folding chair.
His mother asked, "Where is Pierre?"
The lion answered, *"I don't care!"*
His father said, "Pierre's in there!"

CHAPTER 5

They rushed the lion into town
The doctor shook him up and down.
And when the lion gave a roar—
Pierre fell out upon the floor.
He rubbed his eyes
and scratched his head
and laughed because he wasn't dead.
His mother cried and held him tight.
His father asked, "Are you all right?"
Pierre said, "I am feeling fine,
please take me home,
it's half past nine."
The lion said, "If you would care
to climb on me, I'll take you there."
Then everyone looked at
Pierre who shouted,
"Yes, indeed I care!"
The lion took them home to rest
and stayed on as a weekend guest.

The moral of Pierre is CARE!

SKILLS activity

MULTIPLE-MEANING WORDS

Some words look and sound alike. But they have different meanings. You have to read the whole sentence to understand how the word is used. This is called reading a word **in context.** Read the sentences below.

> Three children tried out for the new <u>play</u>.
> I like to <u>play</u> outside.

In the first sentence <u>play</u> means a story people act out. In the second sentence <u>play</u> means to have fun. The word <u>play</u> has multiple meanings or more than one meaning.

ACTIVITY A   Read each sentence. Then read each set of meanings. Choose the correct meaning for the underlined word. Write that meaning on your paper.

1. Jane is the <u>star</u> of the play.

   A **star** is a bright light in the sky.
   A **star** is a famous person.

2. The <u>set</u> for our play looks like the inside of a ship.

   A **set** is the scenery and the objects on a stage for a play.
   A **set** is a group of parts that go together.

3. Raise your <u>right</u> arm in the air.

   To be **right** is to be correct.
   Right is the opposite side of left.

4. She had to <u>act</u> like an old woman in the play.

   To perform on stage for an audience is to **act.**
   A division in a play is called an **act.**

5. Turn on the <u>light</u> so we can read.

   A **light** is something that helps people see.
   If something is **light** it is not heavy.

6. Billy used a <u>comb</u> on his hair after it became windblown.

   A **comb** is used to smooth the hair.
   A **comb** is the thick red crest on a rooster's head.

7. I have a grandmother who lives in the <u>country</u>.

   The **country** is the land outside of cities and towns.
   A **country** is an area of land that has borders and a government shared by all the people.

ACTIVITY B Now go back to each set of word meanings in **A.** Find the word and its meaning that you did <u>not</u> use. Write a sentence on your paper using each word in context.

MUSIC, MUSIC FOR EVERYONE
VERA B. WILLIAMS

The young people who performed in the Broadway musical *Really Rosie* worked hard to make the show "theirs." In this story, a musician and her friends form the Oak Street Band. They use their talents to entertain others and to earn money as well.

Our big chair often sits in our living room empty
now. When I first got my accordion, Grandma and
Mama used to sit in that chair together to listen to
me practice. And every day after school while Mama
was at her job at the diner, Grandma would be sitting
in the chair by the window. Even if it was snowing
big flakes down on her hair, she would lean way out
to call, "Hurry up, Pussycat, I've got something nice
for you."

But now Grandma is sick. She has to stay
upstairs in the big bed in Aunt Ida and Uncle Sandy's
extra room. Mama and Aunt Ida and Uncle Sandy and
I take turns taking care of her. When I come home
from school, I run right upstairs to ask Grandma if
she wants anything. I carry up the soup Mama has
left for her; I water her plants and report if the
Christmas cactus has any flowers yet. Then I sit on
her bed and tell her about everything.

Grandma likes it when my friends Leora, Jenny,
and Mae come home with me because we play music
for her. Leora plays the drums. Mae plays the flute,
Jenny plays fiddle and I play my accordion. One time
we played a dance for Grandma that we learned in the
music club at school.

Grandma clapped until it made her too tired. She told us it was like the music in the village where she lived when she was a girl. It made her want to dance right down the street. We had to keep her from trying to hop out of bed to go to the kitchen to fix us a treat.

Leora and Jenny and Mae and I left Grandma to rest and went down to get our own treat. We squeezed together into our big chair to eat it.

"It feels sad down here without your grandma," Leora said. "Even your big money jar up there looks sad and empty."

"Remember how it was full to the top and I couldn't even lift it when we bought the chair for my mother?" I said.

"Remember how it was more than half full when you got your accordion?" Jenny said.

"I bet it's empty now because your mother has to spend all her money to take care of your grandma till she gets better. That's how it was when my father had his accident and couldn't go to work for a long time," Mae said.

Mae had a dime in her pocket and she dropped it into the jar. "That will make it look a little fuller anyway," she said as she went home.

But after Jenny and Leora and Mae went home, our jar looked even emptier to me. I wondered how we would ever be able to fill it up again while Grandma was sick. I wondered when Grandma would be able to come downstairs again. Even our beautiful chair with roses all over it seemed empty with just me in the corner of it. The whole house seemed so empty and so quiet.

I got out my accordion and I started to play. The notes sounded beautiful in the empty room. One song that is an old tune sounded so pretty I played it over and over. I remembered what my mother had told me about my other grandma and how she used to play the accordion. Even when she was a girl not much bigger than I, she would get up and play at a party or a wedding so the company could dance and sing. Then people would stamp their feet and yell, "More, more!" When they went home, they would leave money on the table for her.

That's how I got my idea for how I could help fill up the jar again. I ran right upstairs. "Grandma," I whispered. "Grandma?"

"Is that you, Pussycat?" she answered in a sleepy voice. "I was just having such a nice dream about you. Then I woke up and heard you playing that beautiful old song. Come. Sit here and brush my hair."

I brushed Grandma's hair and told her my whole idea. She thought it was a great idea. "Tell the truth, Grandma," I begged her. "Do you think kids could really do that?"

"I think you and Jenny and Leora and Mae could do it. No question. No question at all," she answered. "Only don't wait a minute to talk to them about it. Go call and ask them now."

And that was how the Oak Street Band got started.

Our music teachers helped us pick out pieces we could all play together. Aunt Ida, who plays guitar, helped us practice. We practiced on our back porch. One day our neighbor leaned out his window in his pajamas and yelled, "Listen, kids, you sound great but give me a break. I work at night. I've got to get some sleep in the daytime." After that we practiced inside. Grandma said it was helping her get better faster than anything.

At last my accordion teacher said we sounded very good. Uncle Sandy said so too. Aunt Ida and Grandma said we were terrific. Mama said she thought anyone would be glad to have us play for them.

It was Leora's mother who gave us our first job. She asked us to come and play at a party for Leora's great-grandmother and great-grandfather. It was going to be a special anniversary for them. It was fifty years ago on that day they first opened their market on our corner. Now Leora's mother takes care of the market. She always plays the radio loud while she works. But for the party she said there just had to be live music.

All of Leora's aunts and uncles and cousins came to the party. Lots of people from our block came too. Mama and Aunt Ida and Uncle Sandy walked down from our house very slowly with Grandma. It was Grandma's first big day out.

There was a long table in the backyard made from little tables all pushed together. It was covered with so many big dishes of food you could hardly see the tablecloth. But I was too excited to eat anything.

Leora and Jenny and Mae and I waited over by the rosebush. Each of us had her instrument all ready. But everyone else went on eating and talking and eating some more. We didn't see how they would ever get around to listening to us. And we didn't see how we could be brave enough to begin.

At last Leora's mother pulled us right up in front of everybody. She banged on a pitcher with a spoon to get attention.

Then she introduced each one of us. "Now we're going to have music," she said. "Music and dancing for everyone."

It was quiet as school assembly. Every single person there was looking right at Leora and Jenny and Mae and me. But we just stood there and stared right back. Then I heard my grandma whisper, "Play, Pussycat. Play anything. Just like you used to play for me."

I put my fingers on the keys and buttons of my accordion. Jenny tucked her fiddle under her chin. Mae put her flute to her mouth. Leora held up her drums. After that we played and played. We made mistakes, but we played like a real band. The little lanterns came on. Everyone danced.

Mama and Aunt Ida and Uncle Sandy smiled at us every time they danced by. Grandma kept time nodding her head and tapping with the cane she uses now. Leora and Jenny and Mae and I forgot about being scared. We loved the sound of the Oak Street Band.

Afterward everybody clapped and shouted. Leora's great-grandfather and great-grandmother thanked us. They said we had made their party something they would always remember. Leora's father piled up plates of food for us. My Mama arranged for Leora, Jenny, and Mae to stay over at our house. When we finally all went out the gate together, late at night, Leora's mother tucked an envelope with our money into Leora's pocket.

As soon as we got home, we piled into my bed to divide the money. We made four equal shares. Leora said she was going to save up for a bigger drum. Mae wasn't sure what she would do with her share. Jenny fell asleep before she could tell us. But I couldn't even lie down until I climbed up and put mine right into our big jar on the shelf near our chair.

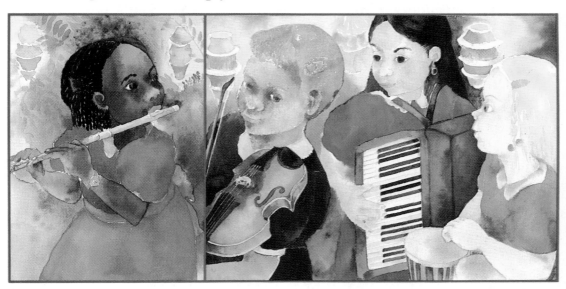

Questions

1. What instruments did the girls play?

2. How did the girl in the story feel about her grandmother? How do you know?

3. Do you think the Oak Street Band will get other jobs? Why or why not?

4. If you were in a band, what instrument would you want to play? Why?

Applying Reading Skills
Figurative Language: Simile

Read each sentence below. Then choose the sentence that has the same meaning.

1. We had to keep Grandma from trying to hop out of bed like a bunny to go fix us a treat.
   a. Grandma wanted to move gently out of her bed.
   b. Grandma wanted to jump right out of her bed.
   c. Grandma jumped so high she could touch the ceiling.

2. We were squeezed like toothpaste into our big chair.
   a. We were too big for our big chair.
   b. We looked like a tube after we sat in the chair.
   c. We were all crammed tightly together in our big chair.

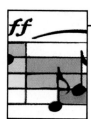

IT'S MUSIC TO MY EARS!

When musicians want to learn a new song, they find a piece of music and read the notes. Often the sheet of music has words, too. Not just the words to a song, but special words at the beginning that tell how to play or sing the notes.

If a song says *allegro* it means you should play it fast. If it says *largo* it should be played slowly. The word *andante* means walking. In music, it means to play at medium speed, not fast, not slow. *Pianissimo* means very softly and quietly. *Fortissimo* means very loud.

All of these words are in the Italian language, but musicians all over the world understand them and perform their music according to the words' directions.

Now that you have learned these musical words, answer these questions.

1. How would you play a lullaby?
2. What would music that was played <u>fortissimo</u> and <u>allegro</u> sound like?
3. How would you play a march?
4. What kind of music would be good to exercise to?
5. How would you feel if you heard music played that was <u>largo pianissimo</u>?

Song of the Empty Bottles

Osmond Molarsky
illustrated by Tom Feelings

In "Music, Music for Everyone," the members of
the Oak Street Band loved to play music. Rosa had her
accordion, Jenny her fiddle, Mae her flute, and Leora
her drums. Thaddeus, the boy in this story, loves
music, too. He often finds himself making up the words
to songs. But more than anything else, Thaddeus longs
for a guitar to play as he sings.

122

Most days, after school, Thaddeus went to the Martin Luther King, Jr. Center, where he fooled around with paints and clay, read books, or just hung out. Nothing doing at home—nobody home. The best day was Thursday, when Mr. Andrews sang songs with his guitar. The other children all sang along, but Thaddeus only pretended. All he wanted was to listen to Mr. Andrews' deep voice and the pling-plung of his guitar.

Sometimes when Thaddeus was alone, he sang to himself—not only the songs Mr. Andrews sang but also songs he made up about himself. Short ones, like:

My mamma goes away all day
But I have this good place to play.

That was when he wished the most to have a guitar of his own, to play when he sang and to make his songs sound like real songs.

Thaddeus loved Mr. Andrews because of his deep voice, but he was too shy to go up front and hang around, like some other children. Then one day between songs, Mr. Andrews looked right at him, standing way in the back, and smiled. That day, Thaddeus stayed after the others left.

"What's your name?" Mr. Andrews asked.

"Thaddeus," he said, and suddenly he no longer felt shy.

"Here," Mr. Andrews said and put the guitar right in his arms.

Thaddeus drew his thumb across the strings four times. Each time, the whole guitar trembled, and inside he trembled with it. He said softly, "How much is a guitar?"

"A guitar costs a bundle," said Mr. Andrews. "Why do you ask?"

"I want to have a guitar," Thaddeus said.

"Think you could learn to play one?"

"Yes."

Mr. Andrews studied him for a while. At last, he said, "I know someone who has a very nice guitar that he will sell for fifteen dollars. Can you get fifteen dollars?"

"I don't know," Thaddeus said, and he got up and walked quickly out of the Center, straight up the hill and home.

When he got there, his little sister, Bernadine, was sitting on the front stoop.

"What are you plotting, Thaddeus?" she said. She could always tell when her big brother had something important on his mind.

"I'm plotting to get a guitar."

"Does Mamma know?"

"Not yet. I just decided."

In a little while, their mother came up the hill, walking slowly. She was tired. "Mamma!" Bernadine screamed. "What do you think? Thaddeus is going to get a real guitar."

"It's only fifteen dollars," Thaddeus said.

"No problem," his mother said. "No problem at all. You just go out and water the little banty tree in the front yard every morning, and in one week, it will be growing five-dollar bills on its branches. Then you can go downtown and buy anything you like. And while you're down there, would you mind picking up a new dress for me? And a pair of shoes?"

Then Thaddeus knew there was no way he could get fifteen dollars from his mother. Not now, not ever. She needed all her money to buy food and stuff.

That next Thursday, Thaddeus waited to talk to Mr. Andrews again. "How do you think I could earn some money?" he asked.

"What about collecting empty bottles?"

"I do that anyway. Everybody does. That's why there's hardly any bottles around. Not enough to get me an ice cream cone. Bottles don't grow on banty trees," he added.

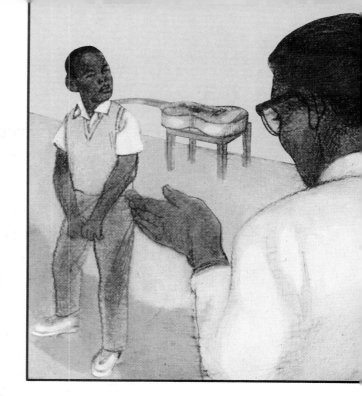

"Come again?" said Mr. Andrews.

"That's a joke."

"I see. Did you ever think of going to the big apartment houses, over on Rhode Island Avenue? I understand people leave bottles in the trash rooms, on every floor. Give it a try. Talk to the doorman. They also leave their newspapers there. Have you got a wagon?"

"An old rickety one."

"A ton of papers is worth nine dollars at the shredders, over on M Street."

"Thanks," said Thaddeus and he took off like a jet for The Oxford House, just around the corner.

The doorman listened to his story and said, "It's all right with me. Leave your wagon in the back, take the service elevator and watch your step. And when you get your guitar, you can sing me a song."

"Thanks," said Thaddeus.

On the following Thursday, Thaddeus was able to report to Mr. Andrews that he had collected five wagonloads of newspapers and twenty-one bottles.

"Great," said Mr. Andrews. "I guess it's time for you to take some guitar lessons. You can start on mine." Now he showed Thaddeus how to hold the guitar with the fingers of his left hand pressing on the strings while he strum-thrummed with his right thumb.

At first, the strings cut into his fingers and hurt. And it was hard to put them where they made the right sound. When he made mistakes, weird sounds bounced off the guitar. But he kept on trying, and every week, after the others went home, Mr. Andrews gave him a lesson.

In time, Thaddeus learned six different ways to put his fingers down on the strings, to make six chords, each different from the others. No matter what note he sang, he could always find a chord to make his own voice sound sweet.

Of course he sang the old songs Mr. Andrews sang, but more than ever, now, Thaddeus was singing songs about himself, like:

It's a hot day, Mr. Fireman,
Please open up the fire hydrant for us.
That'll cool us down, Mr. Fireman,
And wash away all the dust.

"It's a neat song," Mr. Andrews said, when Thaddeus sang it for him. "Maybe someday you'll make up a whole song, hm?"

Thaddeus thought about that for a while, then said, "Yes. Maybe I will."

Every few days now, Thaddeus dumped his money out on his bed and counted it up. The pile was growing, and after only five weeks, he already had four dollars and seventy cents. That came out to almost a dollar a week. In ten more weeks, if he didn't spend any on stuff to eat, he would have fifteen dollars.

"I wish it was ten weeks, already," he said to Mr. Andrews.

"Then you wouldn't have anything to look forward to, would you?"

"I'd have my guitar."

"You win," said Mr. Andrews.

Then one Friday afternoon, he went, as usual, to the Oxford House, to collect a load of papers and a few bottles. There, the super, who lived in the basement, at the back, would not let him in. "Can't have you in the building, kid," he said.

Thaddeus left and went to the Cambridge House. "No boys allowed inside," the super said. "Get lost."

It was the same at the Eaton House, the Rugby House, the Wiltshire Apartments and the Hampshire House. "Go away. No boys allowed." That was the story everywhere.

At the Embassy Gardens, the super said, "Sorry, young fella. Can't let you in."

"Why not?" Thaddeus asked, at last.

"Robberies," the super explained.

"Oh," said Thaddeus. "Hey! I'm not a robber!"

"Maybe you're not, but those are my orders. Sorry. Don't want to lose my job."

Thursday, Thaddeus went to the Center and, after the singing, started to leave with the others.

"Wait, Thaddeus!" Mr. Andrews called to him. "Aren't you going to take your lesson today?"

"I don't feel like it." Thaddeus said.

"What's wrong?" Mr. Andrews looked worried.

"Nothing much."

"Come on, now. Tell me. I want to know."

Thaddeus told him about the robberies, and then he said, "Now I don't think I can ever save fifteen dollars."

Mr. Andrews did not say anything, just strummed some quiet chords on his guitar. He was thinking. Finally, he said, "I want you to try making up a whole song, like 'Where Have All the Flowers Gone?' or 'My Darling Clementine.' I think you could do it."

Thaddeus shrugged. He could not see what good that would do—if he had no guitar.

"Whenever I hear a new song, I write it down," Mr. Andrews explained. "That way I can save it and sing it whenever I want to. Here's what I'll do. If you make up a regular song and it's any good, I'll pay you ten dollars for it. Is that a deal?"

"Oh, wow!" thought Thaddeus. Ten dollars for a song? It would take two hundred empty bottles to get ten dollars. Or sixty wagons full of old newspapers. A song was something you couldn't even see or touch. How could it be worth ten dollars? Well, if Mr. Andrews said so, then it must be so. "Thanks," he said.

Thaddeus walked home thinking he could make up a song that very night, while he was falling asleep. Until now, whenever he made up a song, it just popped into his head. He might be walking down the street and notice something, and suddenly it was a song. Like open fireplugs on a hot day. But now, when he set his mind to making a song, nothing happened. No matter how hard he tried, day or night, walking, running, standing still or lying down, no song would come to him. He even tried standing on his head, but it was no good. What he thought was going to be an easy ten dollars now seemed far, far away. Did Mr. Andrews know this? He really wondered. And so Thaddeus went back to collecting bottles. Determined to get his guitar if it took forever, he looked for bottles wherever he could find them.

Collecting was slow—this was going to take at least a year. Then suddenly, on the fifth day, when he had found only seven bottles, he realized that he was singing, making a song, a brand-new song—a song about what? About bottles! Little by little, the song came into his head. The first bit came when he saw three bottles on a high wall, and he had to wait for a tall man to reach them down for him. "I saw three bottles on a high wall. I wished that I was six feet tall," he sang to himself. "Maybe this is the beginning of a real song," he thought. Another time, he put seven bottles on the kitchen table, poured water into them, to different levels, and tapped them with a spoon. "Ho!" thought Thaddeus. "Another verse!" And he sang, "Tapped some bottles with my spoon and got this funny little tune." Making a song was getting to be easy, and before he had found many more bottles, he had enough verses for a whole song.

Once again it was Thursday afternoon. "I have a surprise, Mr. Andrews," Thaddeus announced. Then he sang his song and strummed chords that made his voice ring out high and sweet.

"Great!" said Mr. Andrews, when he had finished, and Thaddeus was happy. Now he was going to get the ten dollars. "Only one thing is missing. Your song has no chorus."

"No chorus?" Thaddeus said.

"Hold on, man! Things aren't all that bad."

Thaddeus looked downcast and miserable.

"Think," said Mr. Andrews. "Where were all the places you found bottles? Do you remember?"

Thaddeus thought. He thought and he remembered. He named the places. On a high wall. By a park bench. In the dark, scary alley.

"I've got it!" Thaddeus said and began to sing, softly, at first. "Bottles in the alley, bottles in the park. If there is a bottle . . ."

"Now you're cooking!" Mr. Andrews cried. "You've got it! Now let's have it again—the whole song."

Then Thaddeus sang his song, and as he sang,
Mr. Andrews quickly drew music lines on a piece of
paper and wrote it all down, the music and the words.
And by the end of the second verse, he was joining
in, with his deep, booming voice, while Thaddeus sang
high and sweetly.

I look for bot-tles ev-'ry-where,

Where I find them I don't care.

Chorus

Bot-tles in the al-ley, Bot-tles in the

park, If there is a bot-tle I can

find it in the dark. Find it in the dark.

I saw three bottles on a high wall,
I wished that I was six feet tall.

I tapped some bottles with my spoon
And got this funny little tune.

I saw a bottle in the lake,
Reached it with a big, long rake.

"What shall we call it?" Mr. Andrews asked when they had finished. "'The Empty Bottles Song'?"

"I like that fine," said Thaddeus, and Mr. Andrews wrote it at the top of the page. And underneath it, he wrote, "Words and music by Thaddeus." Then he took ten one dollar bills out of his billfold and handed them to the song writer.

"Just a minute," Mr. Andrews said, and he went out to his car, while Thaddeus emptied his jar of money on a chair, counted out five dollars in nickels and dimes, and put it with the ten bills he had just earned.

Now Mr. Andrews brought the guitar in, handling it with great care, and polishing it up with his handkerchief. Thaddeus could hardly wait to hold it. "Here's the fifteen dollars, Mr. Andrews."

"Thank you. Here is your guitar."

How cool and smooth it felt, and it shone like a mirror. Thaddeus drew his thumb softly across the

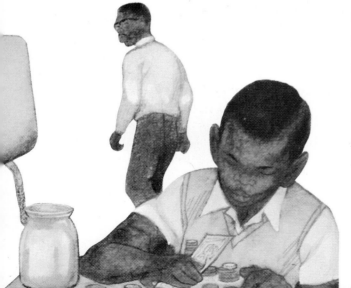

strings. The sounds peeled off sweeter than honey. It was smaller and lighter than Mr. Andrews' guitar, just the right size for a boy. Its voice was softer too, the sweetest sound Thaddeus had ever heard.

He carried it home more carefully than he would carry a half dozen eggs. He walked fast, but he did not run. He picked his feet up at curbs, so he would not trip. At last, he reached the iron gate to his yard and was relieved to see the little banty tree and the front stoop. His guitar was safe.

Thaddeus set his guitar down carefully on the kitchen table. He was thirsty and drank a whole glass of water. Then he poured one on the banty tree. Maybe it was thirsty, too.

He sat down on the front stoop and right off played "Bluetail Fly." Then he played "Oh, Susanna!" and "Go Down Moses." Soon, people sitting in their windows and on their stoops, across the street, were singing along with him. When Bernadine came home, she listened for a minute, just outside the gate. Then she came in, sat down next to her big brother and joined in the singing.

It was getting close to six. Any minute now, their mother would be coming up the hill from work, out of breath and tired, carrying a bag of groceries. Thaddeus was playing a song the neighbors did not know. But soon, they were catching on to the chorus and singing along.

Bottles in the alley, bottles in the park,
If there is a bottle, I can find it in the dark.
It was THE EMPTY BOTTLES SONG!

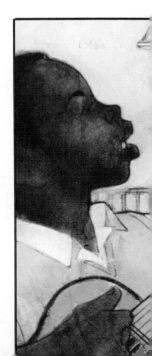

Pretty soon, looking up from the strings that he was strumming, he saw his mother listening by the gate, as he sang and strummed.

I saw a bottle in the lake,
Reached it with a big, long rake.

Then everyone in the neighborhood joined in the chorus. It sounded great.

"I see you got that guitar, after all," said his mother, as she came through the gate.

"Yes, Mamma."

"Where did you get all that money to buy it with?"

Thaddeus wanted to say, "I picked it off the little banty tree, Mamma." But he held back and only said, "Collecting stuff. And Mr. Andrews paid me ten dollars for making a song."

"Ten dollars! For a song? Boy, all I can say is you will come to a good end or a bad end, one or the other. You mark my words. Now you go right on singing and playing that guitar for the neighbors. I'll listen from inside. I'm going to fix some supper." Thaddeus drew his thumb over the strings three times, then began to sing—a brand new song. He was very hungry. This was the way it started:

Pancakes, cornflakes, squash, and cherries,
Pickles, lemons, beans, and berries.

This is the food I love to eat.
I don't care if it's sour or sweet.

Grapes and apples, bread and honey,
Stew and chicken, chocolate money.

This is the food I love to eat.
I don't care if it's sour or sweet.

His mother was calling him now. After dinner, he would make up more words for the new song. Then on Thursday he could sing it for Mr. Andrews.

138

Questions

1. What happened every Thursday afternoon at the Martin Luther King, Jr. Center?

2. Why did Mr. Andrews help Thaddeus get the money for the guitar by offering ten dollars for a song?

3. Do you think Thaddeus had a natural talent for playing the guitar and making up songs? Why or why not?

4. Make up a verse to add to "The Empty Bottle Song."

Applying Reading Skills
Draw Conclusions

Read each conclusion below. Then write two or three sentences that give information to support the conclusion.

1. Thaddeus really didn't care very much about collecting empty bottles.

2. Thaddeus really wanted to learn to play the guitar.

3. Collecting bottles gave Thaddeus the idea for the song.

4. Thaddeus worked hard thinking up verses for his song.

WRITING activity

DESCRIPTIVE PARAGRAPH

Prewrite

In "The Song of the Empty Bottles," Thaddeus used words and music to tell about or describe something he liked to do, search for bottles. You are going to write a paragraph that describes a game or sport you like.

To get your thinking started, copy the word map below on your paper. Add to this word map. Ask your teacher and friends to help. Notice that the words are in different categories. What categories can you add to the map? What words can you add in each category?

FEELINGS	ACTIONS	IDEAS	NAMES
excited	leap	contest	basketball
brilliant	bounce	exercise	kickball
flashing	wobble	compete	baseball
terrific			running
			gymnastics
			dancing
			skating

GAMES AND SPORTS

Now choose a game or sport as a subject for your paragraph. Circle on your word map all the words you might use to describe your subject.

140

Write

1. Think about your subject. In your paragraph you need to tell:
   - the name of the game or sport
   - directions for the game or sport
   - your feelings about the game or sport
2. Think about the order of events in your paragraph. What will you talk about first, last?
3. Your first sentence must make your reader want to go on reading. For example: As you flash across the silver ice on your skates, you feel like a speeding comet.
4. Try to use words from your word map in your paragraph.
5. Now write the first draft of your paragraph.

Revise

Read your paragraph. Have a friend read it, too. Think about this checklist as you revise.

1. Would the readers of your paragraph know enough about your subject to do it themselves? Do you need to add anything to the directions?
2. Which words help your readers know your feelings? Could you find better words?
3. Check your spelling and punctuation.
4. Now rewrite your paragraph to share.

A Bowl of Sun

Frances Wosmek

Thaddeus reached his goal with the help of a new friend. Megan, the girl in this story, moves from a small town to a large city. The change is especially difficult for her to make because she is blind. Then Megan finds a friend who teaches her to do something special. She discovers a talent in herself that gives her new confidence.

For a long time Megan had not even known that she was blind. Outside the house, Mike's firm, strong hand had taught her how to move from here to there, from this place to that. Inside the house she knew just where everything was. She could easily find her way alone from her own small room with its soft bed, through the living room, and on out to the front where Mike had his shop.

Mike was her father. He worked very hard cutting and stitching his fine new leather. From the leather he made belts, sandals, and bags. These he sold in his shop.

Megan liked being near Mike as he worked. She kept the shop tidy, sweeping up the scraps of leather that fell to the floor.

On Sunday afternoons, they walked down to the seashore. It was only a short walk to the water.

The cold water slid over their bare feet. Megan scooped big handfuls of the fine sand. She parted her fingers slowly, feeling the sand trickle through in a thin stream. Together they built a wonderful sand castle with great tall towers and bridges and moats.

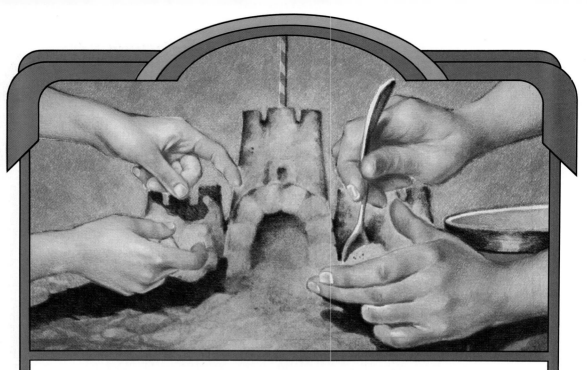

A long time ago Mike had told her about castles.
He had held Megan's hand in his, moving it over the
sand. He helped her mold the wet sand until she had
learned to make the shapes he told her about.

Megan stroked and patted the cool, damp sides of
the castle until they were nearly as smooth as Mike's
leather.

"The sun will soon be gone," Mike said at last.
"It is time to go home. The sky is getting pink. Pink
as a rose."

Megan smiled. She knew that pink was a happy
color. The sound of Mike's voice told her that. She
remembered the smell of a rose. It must be a very
happy sky, she thought. She put her hand in Mike's
and they started for home.

Then, one day, Megan's familiar world suddenly turned upside down. "We are going to move," Mike told her. "We are moving to Boston. There is a special school for you there."

Before Megan knew what was happening, everything was arranged. Mike said he would work in a leather shop in Boston. He and Megan would live in a big house that Mike had found close by the new shop.

There was nothing Megan could do. Everything seemed to happen so fast. She felt lost in a whirl of packing boxes, moving vans, and good-byes. The things and the people she had always known seemed to melt away. The sound and smell of the ocean faded into the distance.

The new world was one of hustle and bustle. The sounds were of traffic, sirens, and strange voices that never stopped. It was a world of unfamiliar spaces and strange objects.

Megan felt alone and helpless. She waited to be taken from this place to that, from her new home to her new school, and back again. She didn't try to do anything by herself.

Mike was worried and upset. "She has never been so helpless," he told Rose. Rose lived in a corner room in the big house. She made clay pots on a wheel to sell, and wove soft things on a big loom.

"Don't worry," said Rose. "It will work out."

But things did not seem to be working out at all. Day after day, when Megan was brought from school, she sat alone by the open window remembering the smell of the sea. She heard the harsh sounds of a busy city and remembered the sound of the waves gently washing up onto the sand.

Sometimes Rose took her to Mike's shop. The smell of the leather was the same, but Mike did not need her now. Somebody else tidied the shop and swept up the scraps.

The teachers at the school shook their heads. "She is no trouble," they told Mike, "but she will not try anything by herself. You must do your best to help."

"Have Rose bring you down to the shop after school," Mike told Megan one morning. "We will go for a walk in the park when I am through working. We will go for a ride on the swan boats."

Megan smiled. "I would like that," she said. It had been a long time since anything had pleased her so much. She and Mike would have fun together—just the two of them! It would be almost like old times.

The day seemed endless. Megan could think of nothing else but Mike, the park, and the mysterious swan boats. School finally dragged to a close. Never had the bus ride home seemed so slow.

At long last, Megan stood before the door of Rose's corner room in the big house. Breathlessly she knocked, then stepped back, waiting for the door to open.

Nothing happened. It was plain that Rose was not there.

Tears began to roll down Megan's cheeks. She felt small, and alone, and very helpless. What could she do? Mike would be waiting. He would be disappointed, too, if she did not come.

Then, in a flash, Megan knew what she must do. She must go alone. It was not very far. She had gone with Rose a number of times. She was quite sure that she remembered the way.

Outside, Megan heard the traffic rolling steadily past the house. She turned in the direction she remembered. She walked carefully and listened for every sound. People hurried by, sometimes brushing her as they passed.

"Watch where you're going!" a boy's voice shouted at her.

Megan began to tremble. Perhaps she had better go back. She was not as sure as she had been that this was the way that Rose had taken her. Then she thought of Mike. He was waiting, and he would be so proud to think that she had found the shop by herself. She walked on.

The curb appeared sooner than she had expected. Before she had time to think, her foot had slipped over the edge. She lost her balance and fell hard. Her knees scraped the rough concrete.

"Watch the light!" someone shouted.

"Look out, little girl, the light is red!" someone else called out.

Confused and frightened, Megan scrambled to her feet as fast as she could. She heard the scream of brakes and the blast of many horns close by. People shouted from every direction. Megan, not knowing which way to turn, stood perfectly still, frozen with fear.

A strong hand grasped Megan's arm and drew her firmly back onto the sidewalk. "There was a red light, little girl. Didn't you see it?" a man's voice asked.

Megan made no reply. Tears were streaming down her cheeks. She was shaking from head to toe.

"No, of course you didn't," the man added more kindly, answering his own question. "Where do you live?"

"I know where she lives," another voice said. "Let me take her home." It was a voice that Megan knew. There was no mistaking Rose's happy voice. Rose took her hand and together they started for home.

Safely back in Rose's quiet room, Megan sat in a big chair while Rose bathed her scraped knees with cool water.

"I called Mike," Rose was saying. "He will take you to the park tomorrow instead."

"Come," she said when she had finished. "I will show you my potter's wheel. If you like, I will teach you how to make a bowl of clay."

Rose's hands guided Megan's over the strange object that was the potter's wheel. Rose was careful to name all its parts, and explained exactly how they all worked together to form the pots and bowls that she made every day.

She put a piece of wet clay into Megan's hands. She showed her how to throw it onto the center of the wheel. She showed her how to start the wheel turning, and how to shape the mound of clay.

Megan held her breath. She forgot the terrifying sounds of traffic that had been ringing in her ears. She forgot her scraped knees. She even forgot about Mike. She felt the cool, damp clay turn beneath her fingers. She imagined a shape and felt it growing under the pressure of her hands. She remembered the sea. She remembered the sand castles that she and Mike had made. She thought of the sun going down in a pink sky.

Then, for a long time, she thought of nothing else but Rose's words and her hands, as they guided and directed her own.

By the end of the afternoon Rose was very pleased. "I never knew anyone who learned so fast," she said in amazement. "There's no mistake about it. You have a natural touch."

"I want to make a bowl for Mike," Megan told Rose, "but it must be a surprise."

Rose smiled. "Every afternoon after school we can work," she said. "I will teach you everything I know."

Megan's world suddenly seemed to be filled with sunshine. All her new experiences began to seem wonderful and exciting.

"I can't believe it," said Mike, shaking his head. "Why should things suddenly change for her?"

Rose smiled, but said nothing. She kept their secret.

The teachers were delighted. "Megan is coming into her own," they all agreed. "Why she seems to be learning faster than we can teach!"

Every afternoon, without fail, Megan sat at Rose's wheel and practiced. The cool clay slipped through her hands and little by little she learned to guide its shape.

Finally Megan and Rose agreed that one of the bowls was better than all the others, and was ready to be finished.

"I will bake it in my kiln," Rose explained. "The heat will make the clay hard. It can have a color, too, if you like."

It took Megan no time at all to decide. "It must be pink," she declared, "as pink as the sky when the sun goes down.

Mike had no idea at all why he was being invited to Rose's room. "It's a surprise," Megan said, "a surprise that Rose and I have been working on for a long time."

When the bowl was placed in Mike's hands, Megan waited breathlessly, eager to hear what he would say.

For what seemed like a very long time he said nothing at all. Then he turned to Rose. "Did she really make this all by herself?" Megan could hear the surprise in his voice.

Rose nodded. "She could be very good, Mike. She seems to know. She hardly needs to be taught."

Mike laid the bowl down carefully. He gripped Megan's shoulders with his big hands. "Someday you will have your own wheel," he said, and his voice trembled a little. "Then, when you are through with school, maybe we can be partners again in a shop beside the sea."

Megan smiled happily. The important feeling was back.

Questions

1. Why did Megan feel helpless when she first moved to Boston?

2. What should Megan do before she tries to go to Mike's shop alone again?

3. Why do you think Megan learned everything Rose taught her so fast?

4. How would you describe your favorite color to someone who was blind?

Applying Reading Skills
Character's Motives or Feelings

Use complete sentences to answer the questions below.

1. How did Megan feel when she first moved to Boston?

2. Why did Megan decide to go alone to her father's shop?

3. How did Megan feel when she started out from Rose's house?

4. How did Megan feel when she began to work with the clay?

5. Why did Megan make a pink bowl?

MA LIEN
and the Magic Brush

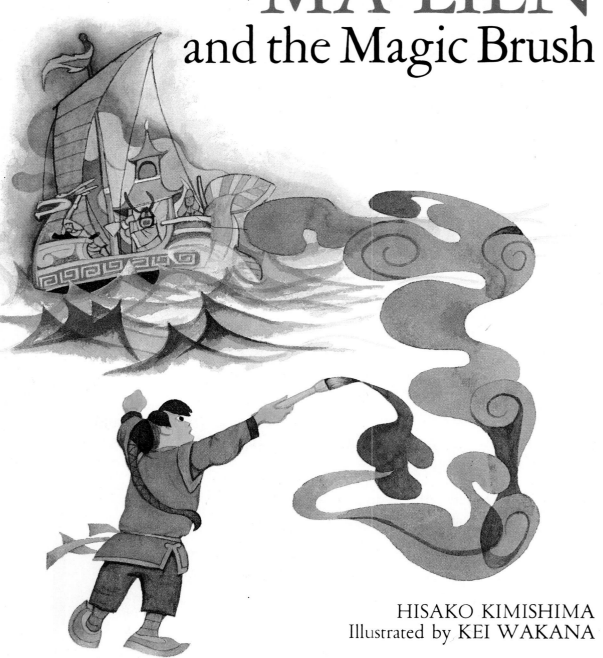

HISAKO KIMISHIMA
Illustrated by KEI WAKANA

Ma Lien, the boy in this Chinese folk tale, has a special talent. His goal is to become an artist and paint beautiful pictures. But he is a poor boy and doesn't have money to buy a paintbrush. Finally, a kind wizard gives Ma Lien a brush of his own—a magic one! Read to see how he uses the magic brush and his artistic gift.

There once lived in China a poor peasant boy named Ma Lien. Day after day he worked hard in the fields so that he would have food to eat and a small hut to live in.

Ma Lien's greatest dream was to be an artist, but the boy had not so much as a copper coin with which to buy a brush.

One day as he trudged along under a heavy load, he passed by the house of a famous artist. Going over the gate in the high wall, Ma Lien peeked in, hoping to see the great man at work.

Silently he stood, watching the artist as he painted a portrait of the mandarin. At last the boy could hold his excitement no longer, and he boldly spoke up. "Oh, great one," he said, "could you let me have one of your brushes—an old one that you don't need anymore—so that I, too, might paint a picture?"

On hearing this unexpected voice the artist turned around. When he saw it was only a poor peasant boy daring to ask for one of his brushes he became very angry.

"Ha, so you think you would like to paint!" he cried. "Away with you and back to your fields!" And he drove the frightened Ma Lien from his gate.

But Ma Lien would not be discouraged. He drew pictures wherever he could, using a stone to scratch on a flat rock, or his fingers to draw in the wet sand of the riverbank.

When he went back to his hut at night, he drew pictures on the wall by the light of a flickering candle. Soon he had covered the walls with pictures of everything he could think of.

With practice, Ma Lien became more and more skillful. One day he drew a picture of a small chicken. A hawk flew by and circled around and around, thinking it was a real chicken. Another time he drew a scowling wolf on a rock in the pasture. The cows and sheep were so frightened by this wolf that they would not go near the rock, even though it was surrounded with lush sweet grass.

But with all his skill, Ma Lien still did not have a brush. Lying one night on his bed he looked around his room at all the pictures he had scratched on the clay walls and sighed.

"Oh, if only I had a brush," he said. "What beautiful pictures I would paint."

With that there was a flash of light, and standing before the boy was an old wizard. He was leaning on a twisted cane, and his white beard fell to the floor.

"Ma Lien," he said in a creaky voice. "You have worked very hard and now you have earned a brush. Use it wisely, for it has great power." And saying this he handed the trembling boy a beautiful paintbrush.

Before Ma Lien could even stammer out a thank you, the old man had vanished.

With a cry of joy the boy rushed over to the one bare spot on his wall and quickly painted a proud and happy rooster. But he had no sooner painted the last curling feather of the rooster's tail when the bird sprang from the wall and flew to the windowsill. There he gave a great *cock-a-doodle-doo* and disappeared into the night.

"Now I know why the wizard said this brush had great power," said Ma Lien. "Do not worry, old man, I *will* use it wisely."

The next morning as Ma Lien was walking to the mountain to gather firewood, he passed a rice paddy. There he saw a man and a young boy pulling a heavy plow to till the paddy. Ma Lien quickly went over to the wall of an old shed and painted a strong and healthy water buffalo. Again, just as he finished, the beast leaped from the wall and with a low *moooo* he lumbered down to the paddy. Now with the help of the buffalo the man and his son soon had the paddy ready for planting.

Just at that moment
the mandarin came by.
Seeing the power of
Ma Lien's magic brush, he
ordered his men to seize the poor boy.

When they had brought Ma Lien to the mandarin,
he commanded the boy to paint a pile of silver coins
for him. Ma Lien, remembering the wizard's words,
refused, and the mandarin had him thrown in the
dungeon with his other prisoners.

Ma Lien soon discovered that the other men had
done no wrong, but had been imprisoned by the
mandarin so that he could steal their lands.

"Never fear," said the boy. "I will have us all
free before too long."

As the night passed, Ma Lien waited until the
guards had dozed off. Then quickly he painted a door
on the wall. The prisoners pushed against it, the door
swung open, and they fled into the night. The
mandarin's men came chasing after Ma Lien, but the
boy easily escaped on the fine horse he had painted
for himself.

Ma Lien knew he would not be safe if he remained on the mandarin's lands, so he rode for many miles until he came to a strange village. Here he continued to help anyone he could with his magic brush.

He painted buffaloes to help the farmers in their fields. He painted toys to keep the children happy.

One day he came upon some farmers hard at work carrying buckets of water to their dried-up fields. "That work is much too hard for you," said Ma Lien, and he set about painting a fine water wheel so that it would be easier to bring the water from the river into the fields.

And so it was that Ma Lien and his wonderful brush became known throughout the land.

It wasn't long before the mandarin learned where Ma Lien was living. He sent his soldiers to the village and when they found the boy they seized him and dragged him back to the palace.

163

The mandarin instantly took away the brush and commanded that the boy be thrown into the dungeon. "Without this I don't think he will escape so easily," he laughed.

Then he sent for the court painter and ordered him to paint a picture with the brush.

"What would you have me paint?" he asked.

"A tree," said the mandarin. "A tree with leaves of gold that will fall like the rain when I shake the branches."

The artist went right to work and soon had a fine tree painted on the wall of the palace. But when the mandarin rushed to shake the tree he got no more than a bump on the head for his trouble. The tree was nothing but a painting on the wall.

Now the mandarin realized that only Ma Lien could paint pictures that would become real. Sending for the boy, he spoke kindly to him.

"Ma Lien," he said softly, "if you will paint but one picture for me I will give you your freedom."

The boy, thinking of a way to trick the greedy man, agreed to do as he was asked.

The mandarin's eyes lit up with delight. He handed the brush to Ma Lien and said, "Paint me a mountain of pure gold." The boy went to work at once, painting a broad expanse of blue sea. The wide sea spread all across the wall.

"Why do you paint the sea?" demanded the mandarin. "I ordered a mountain of gold."

"I have not finished," said the boy quietly, and with that he painted a great gold mountain rising up out of the sea.

"Beautiful, beautiful!" cried the man. "Now paint me a ship so that I can sail to my mountain and bring back the gold."

In a twinkling Ma Lien had painted a fine ship, worthy of a mandarin who was about to travel to a mountain of gold.

The man wasted
no time in hurrying
aboard with a troop of his
finest soldiers. The sail was
raised and slowly the ship rode out to sea.

"Too slow, too slow!" shouted the mandarin.
"Give us a wind to speed us along."

Obediently, Ma Lien painted a wind cloud. The
wind came whistling down and the sails filled out. The
wind ruffled the water and great waves rose about the
ship.

"Too much!" cried the mandarin angrily. "You will
sink my ship."

But Ma Lien payed no attention. He went right
on painting storm clouds. Now the wind howled and
shrieked, and the waves crashed about the ship. Then
with a great *crrrack*, the ship split in two and sank in
the stormy waters.

Once more Ma Lien returned to his simple life
with the peasants, always ready to help them with
their work. And never again was he forced to use his
magic brush for evil and greed.

Questions

1. What happened when Ma Lien asked the famous artist for a brush?

2. How do you know Ma Lien was a skillful artist, even without a brush?

3. Do you think Ma Lien used the brush wisely? Why or why not?

4. If you had the magic brush, how would you use it to help people?

Applying Reading Skills
Draw Conclusions

Read each conclusion below. Then write two or three sentences that give information to support the conclusion.

1. The mandarin was afraid of Ma Lien's power.

2. Ma Lien thought that it was important to help people with his brush.

3. Ma Lien wanted to learn to paint more than anything else in the world.

4. The mandarin didn't understand the greatness of Ma Lien's power.

Pad and Pencil

I drew a rabbit. John erased him
and not the dog I said had chased him.

I drew a bear on another page,
but John said, "Put him in a cage."

I drew some mice. John drew the cat
with nasty claws. The mice saw that.

I got them off the page real fast:
the things I draw don't *ever* last.

We drew a bird with one big wing:
he couldn't fly worth anything,

but sat there crumpled on a limb.
John's pencil did a job on *him*.

Three bats were next. I made them fly.
John smudged one out against the sky

above an owl he said could hoot.
He helped me with my wolf. The brute

had lots too long a tail, but we
concealed it all behind a tree.

By then I couldn't think of much
except to draw a rabbit hutch;

but since we had no rabbit now
I drew what must have been a cow,

with curvy horns stuck through the slats—
they both looked something like the bats.

And feeling sad about the bear
inside his cage, I saw just where

I'd draw the door to let him out.
And that's just all of it, about.

David McCord

169

DRAW CONCLUSIONS

Sometimes an author chooses not to tell you everything about the story. Instead, you must figure out what happened and why. This is called **drawing conclusions.** When you draw conclusions, you think about what you already know and then compare it to the information in the story.

ACTIVITY Read each paragraph about some of the characters in your stories. Answer the question about what happened. Then answer the question about how you drew the conclusion. Write your answers on your paper.

Mr. Andrews, the music teacher, had promised Thaddeus ten dollars if Thaddeus would write him a song. Thaddeus knew he could make up a song without really trying. He might be walking down the street and see something and make up a song about it. But tonight, when he really needed a song, he couldn't think of anything. He kept trying and trying.

Why couldn't Thaddeus think of a song?

a. He was trying too hard.
b. He was too busy doing his homework.
c. He didn't know how.

You know that Thaddeus wanted to write the song

a. because he went to the game instead.
b. because he kept trying and trying.
c. because he wanted to be famous.

Ma Lien had a magic brush that made whatever he painted become real. Once he saw a hungry hawk about to swoop down and catch a tiny mouse. He painted a picture of a hole in the ground. The hawk flew away to look for food elsewhere.

What happened to the Mouse?

a. It hopped onto the paintbrush and escaped.
b. The hawk ate it.
c. The mouse ran into the hole.

How did you know that the mouse was saved?

a. The hawk was still looking for food.
b. The hawk tried to fit into the hole, but couldn't.
c. The mouse was laughing.

Miss Rumphius

Barbara Cooney

Ma Lien used his magic brush to help others and make his world better. In this story, an artist challenges his granddaughter, Alice, to do something to make the world more beautiful. She agrees, but first she has to find out what that could be.

The Lupine Lady lives in a small house overlooking the sea. In between the rocks around her house grow blue and purple and rose-colored flowers. The Lupine Lady is little and old. But she has not always been that way. I know. She is my great-aunt, and she told me so.

Once upon a time she was a little girl named Alice, who lived in a city by the sea. Many years ago her grandfather had come to America on a large sailing ship.

Now he worked in the shop at the bottom of the house, making figureheads for the prows of ships. For Alice's grandfather was an artist. He painted pictures, too, of sailing ships and places across the sea. When he was very busy, Alice helped him put in the skies.

In the evening Alice sat on her grandfather's knee and listened to his stories of faraway places. When he had finished, Alice would say, "When I grow up, I too will go to faraway places, and when I grow old, I too will live beside the sea."

"That is all very well, little Alice," said her grandfather, "but there is a third thing you must do."

"What is that?" asked Alice.

"You must do something to make the world more beautiful," said her grandfather.

"All right," said Alice. But she did not know what that could be.

In the meantime Alice got up and washed her face and ate porridge for breakfast. She went to school and came home and did her homework.

And pretty soon she was grown up.

Then my Great-aunt Alice set out to do the three things she had told her grandfather she was going to do. She left home and went to live in another city far from the sea and the salt air. There she worked in a library, dusting books and keeping them from getting mixed up, and helping people find the ones they wanted. Some of the books told her about faraway places.

People called her Miss Rumphius now.

Sometimes she went to the conservatory in the middle of the park. When she stepped inside on a wintry day, the warm moist air wrapped itself around her, and the sweet smell of jasmine filled her nose.

"This is *almost* like a tropical isle," said Miss Rumphius. "But not quite."

So Miss Rumphius went to a real tropical island, where people kept cockatoos and monkeys as pets. She walked on long beaches, picking up beautiful shells. She climbed tall mountains where the snow never melted. She went through jungles and across deserts. She saw lions playing and kangaroos jumping. And everywhere she made friends she would never forget. Finally she came to the Land of the Lotus-Eaters, and there, getting off a camel, she hurt her back.

"What a foolish thing to do," said Miss Rumphius. "Well, I have certainly seen faraway places. Maybe it is time to find my place by the sea."

And it was, and she did.

From the porch of her new house, Miss Rumphius watched the sun come up; she watched it cross the heavens and sparkle on the water; and she saw it set in glory in the evening. She started a little garden among the rocks that surrounded her house, and she planted a few flower seeds in the stony ground. Miss Rumphius was *almost* perfectly happy.

"But there is still one more thing I have to do," she said. "I have to do something to make the world more beautiful."

But what? "The world already is pretty nice," she thought, looking out over the ocean.

The next spring Miss Rumphius was not very well. Her back was bothering her again, and she had to stay in bed most of the time.

The flowers she had planted the summer before had come up and bloomed in spite of the stony ground. She could see them from her bedroom window, blue and purple and rose-colored.

"Lupines," said Miss Rumphius with satisfaction. "I have always loved lupines the best. I wish I could plant more seeds this summer so that I could have still more flowers next year."

But she was not able to.

After a hard winter spring came. Miss Rumphius was feeling much better. Now she could take walks again. One afternoon she started to go up and over the hill, where she had not been in a long time.

"I don't believe my eyes!" she cried when she got to the top. For there on the other side of the hill was a large patch of blue and purple and rose-colored lupines!

"It was the wind," she said as she knelt in delight. "It was the wind that brought the seeds from my garden here! And the birds must have helped!"

Then Miss Rumphius had a wonderful idea!

She hurried home and got out her seed catalogues. She sent off to the very best seed house for five bushels of lupine seed.

All that summer Miss Rumphius, her pockets full of seeds, wandered over fields and headlands, sowing lupines. She scattered seeds along the highways and down the country lanes. She flung handfuls of them around the schoolhouse and back of the church. She tossed them into hollows and along stone walls.

Her back didn't hurt any more at all.

The next spring there were lupines everywhere. Fields and hillsides were covered with blue and purple and rose-colored flowers. They bloomed along the highways and down the lanes. Bright patches lay around the schoolhouse and back of the church. Down in the hollows and along the walls grew the beautiful flowers.

Miss Rumphius had done the third, the most difficult thing of all!

My Great-aunt Alice, Miss Rumphius, is very old now. Her hair is very white. Every year there are more and more lupines. Now they call her the Lupine Lady. Sometimes my friends stand with me outside her gate, curious to see the old, old lady who planted the fields of lupines. When she invites us in, they come slowly. They think she is the oldest woman in the world. Often she tells us stories of faraway places.

"When I grow up," I tell her, "I too will go to faraway places and come home to live by the sea."

"That is all very well, little Alice," says my aunt, "but there is a third thing you must do."

"What is that?" I ask.

"You must do something to make the world more beautiful."

"All right," I say.

But I do not know yet what that can be.

Questions

1. How does the narrator know Miss Rumphius, or the Lupine Lady?

2. Why was making the world more beautiful the hardest of the three things Miss Rumphius had to do?

3. Do you think lupines grow easily, or need a lot of care? Explain your answer.

4. What would you do to make the world more beautiful?

Applying Reading Skills
Multiple-Meaning Words

Use context clues to choose the correct meaning of each underlined word. Write each word and its meaning.

1. The warm moist air wrapped itself around Miss Rumphius.
   - a. to cover with paper
   - b. to cover
   - c. to fold
   - d. to conceal

2. Miss Rumphius saw a large patch of blue and purple and rose-colored lupines.
   - a. a piece of material
   - b. a small piece of ground
   - c. an eye pad
   - d. a part of the shore

Barbara Cooney

"My father was a stockbroker, my mother painted pictures for fun; so her children did too, and that's how it all began."

Barbara Cooney doesn't recall deciding to become an artist. "As far back as I can remember," she says, "I could always entertain myself by drawing pictures." Cooney was lucky that her mother could always supply her with the materials she needed.

Like most artists, Cooney has many interests. Where does she get her ideas? "I might get interested in the woods, France or Spain, or life in the Middle Ages, or mice, say, and then the ideas come. Some of my texts take reworking, sometimes much, sometimes little." The idea for *Chanticleer and the Fox*, for example, came because "I just happened to want to draw chickens." Out of such interest have come the illustrations for over sixty books!

More to Read   *Chanticleer and the Fox*
The Little Juggler

183

Reach Out

The stories in *Reach Out* are about characters who had goals and dreams. The characters worked hard and succeeded in making their dreams become real. Each person turned their dreams into reality by reaching out for the help of a friend or family member.

Thinking About *Reach Out*

1. How did Miss Rumphius in "Miss Rumphius" and Ma Lien in "Ma Lien and the Magic Brush" help make their worlds better?

2. What was Katy's goal on the camping trip in "Katy Did It"? Who helped her reach that goal?

3. How did a love of music help Rosa in "Music, Music for Everyone" and Thaddeus in "The Song of the Empty Bottles" make their dreams come true?

4. Why didn't Angelina in "Lorenzo and Angelina" reach her goal of seeing the world from the top of El Padre Mountain?

5. Write about a special goal you would like to reach. Tell about the ways you will make your dream a reality.

Introducing Level 9
Unit 2
Snails To Whales

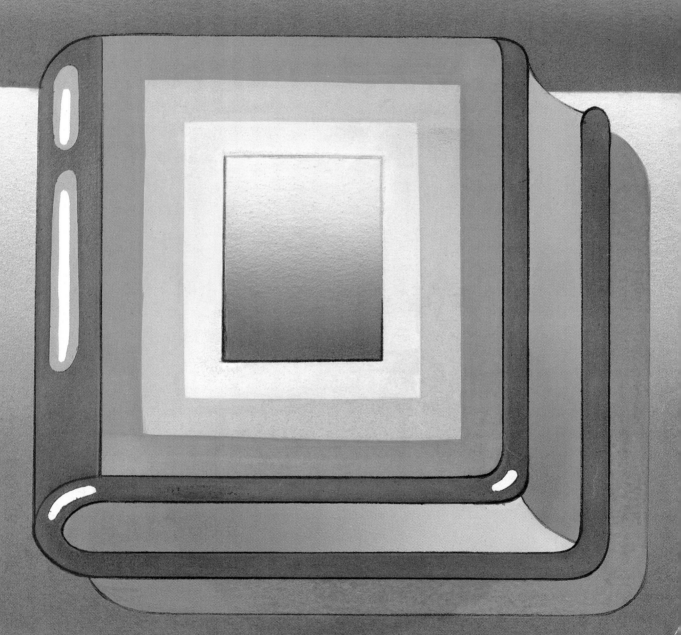

SECRETS OF A
WILDLIFE
WATCHER

WRITTEN AND ILLUSTRATED BY

JIM ARNOSKY

Watching is the best way to learn about animals and how they live. By watching, you can find out how animals move, build homes, hunt, and eat. In this guide, Jim Arnosky, an artist and naturalist, reveals his secrets of watching wildlife.

The woods were very wet. Dirt gurgled under the press of my feet as I walked a familiar trail. I was wide-eyed for the sight of wildlife. Ahead, something moved on the wet leaves. It was a little snake! I tried to get a closer look. But it moved behind a fallen tree branch. I approached again, very slowly. I knelt a few feet from the broken branch. The snake didn't move. It was an olive-colored garter snake with bright yellow stripes down its back. Its eyes were like polished stones. I wondered what the snake was seeing. Its delicate head was jade green and its mouth white. A tiny forked tongue flicked out. It was deep red.

The little snake had sensed my approach. It was seeking cover when I spotted it. Once behind the branch it felt hidden. So it stayed, even when I came near. One secret to getting close to small or shy animals is to let them find cover before trying to approach them.

Wild animals are sensitive to everything around them. Stalking them takes practice and patience. In reptiles, fish, and mammals, the sense of smell is sharp. A snake needs its sense of smell to find food and sniff out danger. A salmon can smell a bear in the water a mile upstream. A fox can sniff a rabbit's scent in tracks that are days old.

Wherever you go, you leave some of your scent in tiny molecules that come from your body

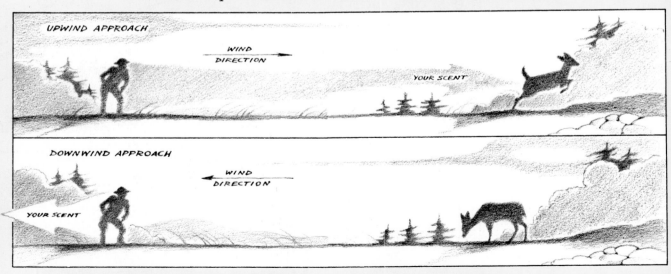

and clothing. Often your scent reaches an animal long before you do and scares it away. When you see a wild animal, stay downwind. This will keep your scent in back of you and away from the animal you are watching.

Most animals can hear as well as they can smell. Even snakes, fish, and others deaf to sounds in the air can feel noises vibrating through the ground. When stalking wildlife, be as quiet as you can.

Step softly. Try not to brush against trees or bushes. If you must make a sound, do so when the animal you are watching is busy chewing food, changing place, or moving to a new spot. It will be making noises of its own. It may not notice yours. If you are heard and the animal becomes alert—freeze in your tracks!

Keep still, and most animals will not see you, even if you are out in the open. Mostly, animals look for movements. Many animals, including most mammals, see only in shades of gray. A motionless figure is hard for them to pick out of a scene. Sometimes the shape of a standing human, still or moving, will frighten them. You can hide your human shape by crouching down.

EVEN IN A MONOCHROME OF GRAYS A STANDING FIGURE IS NOTICEABLE

WHEN CROUCHED DOWN YOU BLEND BETTER WITH THE SCENERY

I once was crouched downwind from a beaver. It was working away on its dam. At times the busy beaver was less than ten feet from me. It rolled some heavy stones to the dam. Then it pushed them into place with the side of its strong body. I could hear the stones squish into the mud on the dam. In my motionless crouch, I was invisible. After a while, though, my legs became stiff. I had to stand and stretch them. At once, the beaver saw me. It disappeared underwater with a loud splash of its flat tail.

ANIMALS WITH POOR VISION — LIKE BEAVERS, MUSKRATS, AND SKUNKS — WILL NOT SEE YOU UNLESS YOU MOVE

A BEAVER ON ALERT

Birds see in color and rely mainly on eyesight for survival. They can see both near and far things much better than other animals. A sparrow's eyes can be focused on a seed right near its beak one second, then focused on a distant cat the next. Flying birds see things up to eight times more sharply than humans do. That's why a hawk high in the sky can spot a mouse running on the ground.

MOST BIRDS CAN WATCH ABOVE FOR DANGER...

AN ANIMAL WHOSE EYES ARE ON THE SIDES OF ITS HEAD CAN SEE NEARLY ALL AROUND WITHOUT TURNING ITS HEAD...

...AND ONE WHOSE EYES ARE FORWARD ON ITS HEAD MUST TURN ITS HEAD TO SEE AROUND

...WHILE SEARCHING BELOW FOR FOOD

Because birds have such fine eyesight, they are hard to approach. Bird watchers use binoculars to study birds. One way to watch them up close without using binoculars is to go to a place they go to often. Sit still, keep quiet, and wait until they come. Soon they will be doing things all around you.

It is possible to get too close to the animals you are watching. Always stay at a distance that is easy for them and for you. Do not disturb nesting birds. And *never* approach an animal that is with its young. Wild animal parents can be very, very protective. If you come upon a baby animal that looks like it's alone, let it be.

Mother may be watching you from a hiding place nearby. Do not touch or corner a wild animal. Never follow an animal into places you don't know. There is no such thing as a tame wild animal. Be careful of any that seem fearless of you. They could be sick and dangerous.

The safest way to get a close look at animals you would not like to go near is to use binoculars. Through these lenses, individual scales, feathers, hairs, and whiskers come into focus.

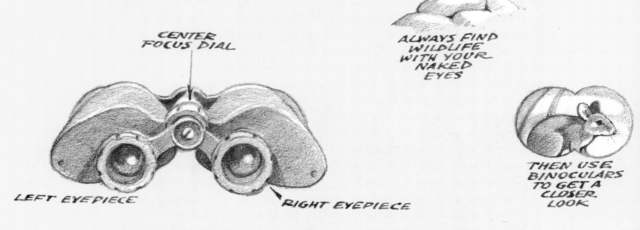

CENTER FOCUS DIAL

ALWAYS FIND WILDLIFE WITH YOUR NAKED EYES

LEFT EYEPIECE

RIGHT EYEPIECE

THEN USE BINOCULARS TO GET A CLOSER LOOK

Everything we know about wildlife was discovered by watching. There is much to learn. Keep a wildlife notebook and write down what you see. Wherever you go there is wildlife to watch. Even in the largest cities, squirrels are sharing trees with bats, birds, and owls. There are pigeons nesting on ledges. Spiders spin webs in windows, and mice run across floors.

All kinds of animals, from mice to moose, have lived parts of their lives with wildlife watchers nearby. I have shared some of my wildlife watching secrets with you. Now take them outside. Use them, and find some secrets of your own. Then pass them along to a friend.

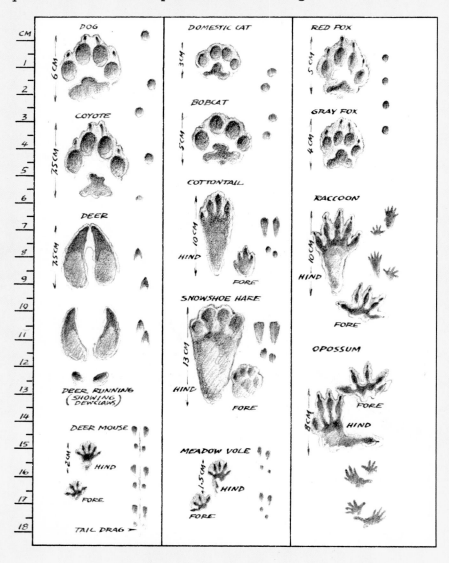

Questions

1. How was Jim Arnosky able to get close to the little snake?

2. Would a beaver or other mammal be frightened by bright colors? Why or why not?

3. Which wildlife-watching secret in the article do you think is most helpful? Explain your answer.

4. What kinds of wildlife would you like to watch more closely? Explain why.

Applying Reading Skills
Main Idea

Read the following paragraph from "Secrets of a Wildlife Watcher." Then write the main idea of the paragraph in your own words.

Most animals can hear as well as they can smell. Even snakes, fish, and others deaf to sounds in the air can feel noises vibrating through the ground. When stalking wildlife, be as quiet as you can.

SKILLS activity

MAIN IDEA

A paragraph is a group of sentences that tell about one subject. The subject of the paragraph is called the **main idea.** Sometimes the main idea of the paragraph is directly stated in one sentence. In other paragraphs, no <u>one</u> sentence gives the main idea. You must read all the sentences to figure out, or **infer** the main idea.

ACTIVITY   Read the following paragraphs. Think about the main idea. Then answer the questions on your paper.

> Step softly. Try not to scrape against trees or brush. If you must make a sound, do so when the animal you are watching is busy chewing food, changing position, or moving to a new spot. It will be making noises of its own. It may not notice yours. If you are heard and the animal becomes alert—freeze in your tracks!

What is the main idea of this paragraph?

a. If you are trying to watch an animal, make as little noise as possible.
b. If you are trying to watch an animal, make all the same noises the animal is making.

196

Bird watchers use binoculars to study birds. One way to watch birds up close without binoculars is to go to a place that they go to often. Sit still, keep quiet, and wait until they arrive. Soon they will be going about their business all around you.

What is the main idea of this paragraph?

a. Birds with fine eyesight stay away from people with binoculars.

b. You can watch birds without binoculars if you wait quietly in a place the birds often go.

Keep still, and most animals will not see you, even if you are out in the open. Usually, animals look for movements. Many animals, including most mammals, see only in shades of gray. A motionless figure is hard for them to pick out of a scene. Sometimes the shape of a standing human, still or moving, will frighten them. You can hide your human shape simply by crouching down.

What is the main idea of this paragraph?

a. Animals will notice you less if you stay low and keep still.

b. Many animals see only grays, not colors.

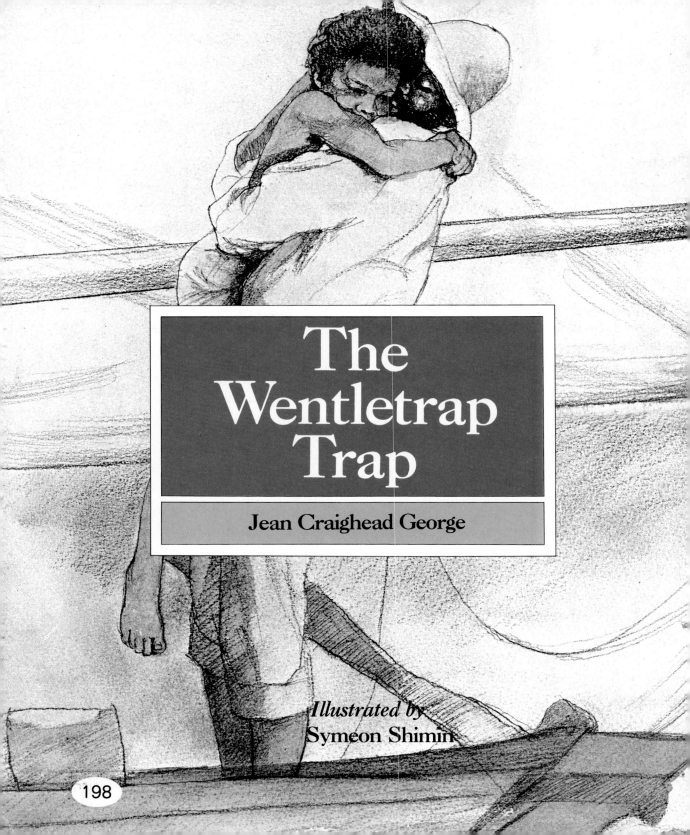

The
Wentletrap
Trap

Jean Craighead George

Illustrated by
Symeon Shimin

To learn about animals, Jim Arnosky got close enough to watch them. Dennis, the boy in this story, lives on an island in the Atlantic Ocean. When a storm threatens the island, Dennis watches and waits to see what the storm—and the ocean—will bring.

Dennis and his father stand on a boat. The boat rocks gently. Red, blue, yellow, and green fish swim in the water.

Dennis and his father live on the island of Bimini. It is a small snip of land in the warm Atlantic Ocean.

"Dennis," says his father, "you must get off the boat now. It's time for me to go to sea."

He picks Dennis up and hugs him. "I must catch plenty of conch to sell to people to use in their soup."

Dennis nods. He knows that.

"And while I am gone," his father begins.

"I know what you are going to say," Dennis says. "'And while I am gone, take good care of yourself.'"

"That's right," says his father, and hugs him again.

Dennis slides down from his arms. He jumps on the dock.

"How can I take care of myself?" he asks. "I don't have a boat or a grapple or a net or a bucket. And I don't have a fine big hat."

"You need a fortune!" says his father. "You'd better gather a ton of seashells to sell to the tourists."

"How could I carry a ton of seashells?"

"Then you'd better find one wentletrap."

"What is a wentletrap?"

His father leans toward him. "A shell so rare that you can swap it for a boat and a grapple and a net and a bucket. You can even get a hat and a shelf of new books to give your mother for her classroom in school."

Dennis looks under the dock. "Where do wentletraps live?"

"At the bottom of the sea. They dwell in dark canyons. They drink sea tea and," he pulls up his knee, "they walk on one foot."

"Is that all?" Dennis asks.

"No, they see only two things. They see white. That's the top of the ocean. And black, that's the bottom of the ocean."

"You tease me!" shouts Dennis. "I can't find a wentletrap. I would need a boat and a grapple and a net and a hat even to get near to a wentletrap."

"No, you wouldn't," says his father. "Just watch the beaches. Great storms tear wentletraps loose from the sea bottom. They carry them up on the beaches and leave them there."

Dennis makes a funny face. "And what, sir," he asks, "does this wentletrap look like?"

"It's so white you suck in your breath when you see it. And so beautiful it makes your skin tingle."

The engine roars. The boat moves. Then it speeds out to sea. Dennis stands alone on the dock.

"Oh, Paw," he cries, "I miss you already."

Dennis jumps to the sand. He hides under the dock.

Time passes.

Hiding makes him feel worse.

"I'm not taking good care of myself," he says out loud.

He crawls into the sunlight. He walks slowly home. Soft trade winds blow.

At dawn he awakens. Sea gulls call. A dog barks. Dennis looks out the window. The sky is dark, the sea is white.

"Storm," Dennis says. "Now is the time to catch a wentletrap."

He picks up an empty box. He puts a few tea leaves into a jar. He opens a drawer and takes out a piece of string. Then he picks up a bright silver coin.

Dennis tiptoes to the door.

"Where are you going?" asks his mother.

He jumps in surprise. "I am going to set a trap for a wentletrap."

His mother shakes her head. "Do not stay long. A bad storm is coming."

203

Dennis walks down the beach. The tide is low. He stares far out at the stormy sea.

"If I were a wentletrap," he says to himself, "and that storm tore me loose, and threw me on shore, what would I do?"

He answers himself. "I would hunt for some sea tea." He puts the jar down on its side next to a conch shell.

"I would look for the sky." He puts the bright coin on the tea jar.

"And I would look for the dark sea bottom." He places the box over the jar.

Then he ties the string to a scallop shell and props the box on the edge of the scallop. He hides himself under a fallen palm leaf nearby.

Dennis is ready to trap a rare wentletrap.

He waits and watches.

"Tap. Tap. Tap." The sound comes from the box.

Dennis pulls. The box falls. He lifts it up. Out walks the tea jar. The jar hurries to the water. The red toes of a hermit crab scutter beneath it.

204

Dennis shakes his fist. He knows all about hermit crabs. They live inside empty seashells. The hard shells protect their soft bodies from harm. As they grow, the hermit crabs hunt for bigger shells. When they find one, they slide their bodies out of the old shells and into the new shells. And they run on their way.

Dennis is mad. "You took my tea jar!" he yells to the hermit crab. "So I'll take your conch shell for my trap."

He sets the trap again. Tap. Tap. Tap. He looks under the box. A moon shell sits where the conch shell sat. The conch shell is running down to the sea. The toes of another hermit crab scutter beneath it.

"Give me my conch shell!" Dennis roars. But this crab disappears too.

"You took my conch shell, so I'll take your moon shell." Dennis peers under the box. Where the moon shell sat, a cone shell sits.

"Okay," Dennis says to the crabs. "I'll make a hermit-proof wentletrap trap."

He ponders a moment. "If I were a wentletrap, I would *not* want tea. I would *not* look for the sky."

He puts the coin back in his pocket. "But I would want to find my dark home. So I would slide right under this box."

Dennis props up the box. He watches and waits. The sky grows dark. Thunder rumbles. The wind whips the sea. Lightning flashes.

Dennis runs to his mother. The rain splashes. Thunder cracks and booms. Dennis curls up in his mother's lap.

"Is Paw all right on the stormy seas?"

She holds him tightly. She does not answer.

The storm rumbles and bangs. At last it growls off like a wounded dog. The rain stops. The sun shines. Water drips softly from leaf and flower. A bird calls.

Dennis slides to the floor.

"I must go check my wentletrap trap," he says to his mother.

She smiles.

He runs down the beach. The tide is high. And the wentletrap trap is under the sea.

"Bah!" cries Dennis. "I will never be able to take good care of myself."

"Dennis!" His mother is calling. "Look what I've found!"

She runs down the beach and sits beside him. "It's an old bottle the storm washed up."

Dennis holds it. He turns it over. He shrugs. He puts the bottle down on the sand.

"Don't you like it?"

"I need a wentletrap," Dennis says, "to swap for a boat and a grapple and a net and a bucket and a hat."

His mother looks up. "Well," she says, "the bottle is not worth a boat or a grapple or a net or a bucket. But you just might swap it for a wonderful hat."

She points down the beach. "Here comes Sinclair. He is wearing a new hat that he made to sell to the tourists."

Sinclair strides toward them. On his head is a hat bright with feathers from parrots and peacocks. It is rimmed with red bottle caps. It is hung with bright pop tops.

On its crown sits a small wooden teacup and a saucer. The hat is a masterpiece.

Dennis runs to meet Sinclair. "Want to swap your hat for an old purple bottle?"

"Sure," says Sinclair. "I can make a new hat, but not an old bottle."

Dennis runs back to his mother. The bottle is gone! A white shell sits there instead.

Dennis is furious. He stamps the ground. He kicks at the hermit in the shell. Then he sucks in his breath. He feels his skin tingle.

"A wentletrap!" Dennis shouts. "I have a wentletrap!"

He leans over the snowy white shell. "Yippee. Hooray."

He turns a cartwheel. "I can, and I will take good care of myself."

He reaches for the wentletrap. It runs to the sea. A wave falls upon it, and the shell disappears.

"Wave!" shouts Dennis, "bring back my wentletrap. Bring it right back to me!"

The wave does not answer.

Dennis throws himself face down on the sand.

"I can't," he sobs. "I just can't take care of myself."

"You don't have to."

Dennis looks up. His father is here. His hat is tipped back at a happy angle. He is hugging Dennis's mother.

"The storm was so bad," he tells Dennis, "that I took good care of myself. I came back to you."

Dennis leaps to his feet. "Hey, Paw," he says. "Let's take good care of our two selves together."

He runs toward the boat, the grapple, the net, and the bucket. Then he thinks of his father's fine big hat.

Dennis stops.

He picks up a teapot. The storm washed it up. He turns it slowly over and over. Then carefully he puts it on his head. He pushes it back at a happy angle.

"Okay," he says to his laughing father. "It's time for me to go to sea."

They run.

A little red foot sticks out of the pot spout.

Questions

1. How did Dennis's father say he could find a wentletrap?

2. Why did Dennis have to make a hermit-proof wentletrap trap?

3. Do you think Dennis really found a wentletrap? Why or why not?

4. Dennis wanted to find a wentletrap to make a fortune. How would you plan to make your fortune?

Applying Reading Skills
Character's Motives or Feelings

Use complete sentences to answer the questions below.

1. Why did Dennis's father go out to sea?
2. How did Dennis feel when his father's boat sped out to sea?
3. Why did Dennis's father return so quickly?
4. How did Dennis feel about losing the wentletrap and why did he feel this way?

THE SNAIL'S SPELL

Imagine
you are soft
and have no bones
inside you.
Imagine
you are grey,
the color of smoke.
You are shrinking
smaller
and
smaller
and
smaller.

You are two inches long,
lying on the brown ground
all soft and grey.
Imagine you have no arms
and legs now.
Imagine you
cannot walk or run.
Instead you glide
and make your own
smooth sticky path
to ride on.
It is easy
to move this way
and it feels
cool and good.
You have a head
and a mouth
with rows of tiny teeth—
but your teeth are on your tongue!

You eat
by sticking out your tongue
and scraping
tiny bits of lettuce
into your tiny mouth.
As you glide slowly
on the damp brown ground,
you touch everything
with two short feelers.
On the top of your head
you have two long feelers.
You can stretch and stretch
these feelers
till they look like
long, long horns.
Your small black eyes
rest at the tips of these feelers.
One eye sees the brightness above.

The other feeler
curls around a lettuce leaf.
Now you can see the darkness there.
But your feeler
touches something in the dark,
something wriggling,
someone alive!
Fast as you can
you pull your feeler back.
You tuck your eye
inside your feeler
and hide it from danger.
Your eye glides
down and down
into your head.
When you feel safe,
your eye glides
up and up
to see your world again.

You are soft and small and slow
gliding up and down
and upside down.
On your back
lies a light, curled shell.
It is part of you
and it grows
as you grow.
Whenever you want to rest,
you have a place to go.
First you tuck your feelers
inside your head.
Then you draw your head
and soft, grey body
inside your shell
and sleep.

Joanne Ryder

A Salmon
for Simon

Betty Waterton

illustrations by Ann Blades

Dennis and his family earned their living from the sea. Simon, the boy in this story, lives on an island near the west coast of Canada. His family fish and clam for food. Simon has been waiting all year to catch a salmon.

All summer Simon had been fishing for salmon.

Last year, when he was little, his sisters had taught him how to catch minnows with a strainer. But this year his father had given him a fishing pole of his own. He had been fishing for a salmon every day.

He hadn't caught a single salmon.

Now it was September. It was the time of the year when many salmon were swimming past the island where Simon lived, near the west coast of Canada. They were returning from the sea, looking for the rivers and little streams where they had been born. There they would lay their eggs so that more salmon could be born.

One day, when the tide was on its way out, Simon and his two sisters went clam-digging. As soon as their pail was full of clams, his sisters took them home to their mother to cook for supper. Simon stayed at the beach. He had his fishing pole with him, as he had every day that summer.

"I'm going to stay and fish for a salmon," he thought. And he did.

He sat on a rock and fished. He sat on a dock and fished. But he didn't even see a salmon.

He stood on the edge of the beach and fished. He saw red and purple starfish sticking to the rocks. He saw small green crabs scuttling among the seaweed. He saw flat white sand dollars lying on the wet sand. He saw pink sea anemones waving, pale jellyfish floating, and shiners swimming.

But he didn't see a salmon.

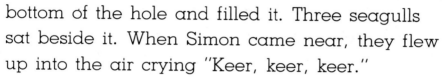

"Is it ever hard to catch a salmon," thought Simon. He decided to stop fishing, maybe forever.

Simon walked back along the beach to the place where he and his sisters had been clam-digging. The sea water had oozed up from the bottom of the hole and filled it. Three seagulls sat beside it. When Simon came near, they flew up into the air crying "Keer, keer, keer."

"I'm not good at catching salmon, but I am a good clam-digger," thought Simon.

He dug a few clams and put them on a nearby rock. The gulls flew down and picked up the clams in their beaks. They carried them into the air and then dropped them. The clams hit the rocks and broke open.

Simon listened to the "bang, bang, pop" of the clam shells as they broke. He watched the gulls fly down and eat the soft clams.

Then Simon heard something different, something sounding like FLAP, FLAP, FLAP.

"What's that?" he cried. Nobody answered.

He heard it again. FLAP, FLAP, FLAP. This time it was right above his head.

The seagulls flew off, calling "Keer, keer, keer." Simon looked up. It was an eagle.

Its wings beat the air FLAP, FLAP, FLAP as it climbed towards the treetops. Simon had often seen bald eagles, but this one was different. It was carrying something in its talons—something that glistened.

"A fish!" cried Simon, "he's got a FISH!"

He was so excited that he began hopping about and flapping his arms like eagles' wings. The seagulls were excited too, and they circled overhead, screeching.

In all the stir and confusion, the eagle
dropped the fish. Down it came out of the sky,

    down
    down
    down
    down
    down

SPLAAT . . . . SPLASH
into the clam hole!

The fish lay on its side in the shallow water
and did not move.

Simon ran over to it. "It's dead," he cried.

Suddenly the fish flicked its tail and flipped
over right side up. Its gills opened and closed
and its fins began to move slowly.

"It's alive," shouted Simon. Then he looked
closer. His eyes grew round. "It's alive and it's a
SALMON," he cried. "It must be the most
beautiful fish in the world," thought Simon.

It was a coho, or silver salmon. It had come
from far out in the Pacific Ocean to find the
stream where it had been born. It had grown big in
the ocean, and strong, and it shone like silver.

All summer Simon had been waiting to
catch just such a fish, and here was one right in
front of him. Yet he didn't feel happy.

He watched the big handsome fish pushing its nose against the gravelly sides of the clam hole. It was trying to find a way out, and he felt sorry for it. He knew it would die if it didn't have enough water to swim in. If only it could get back to the sea, it would live.

Simon wanted the salmon to be safe in the sea where it could swim and leap and dive. And where it would one day find its own stream. He didn't know how he was going to save the salmon. But he had to find a way.

"I won't let you die, Sukai," said Simon. (Sukai was an old Indian name for the salmon. It meant "king of the fishes.")

Simon thought of carrying the fish to the sea, but he knew it was too big and heavy and too slippery for him to pick up.

He thought about waiting for the tide to come in, but he knew the salmon couldn't wait that long.

He looked up at the watching seagulls, but all they said was "Keer, keer."

He MUST find a way.

Looking around, he saw his clam shovel. An idea popped into Simon's head.

He would dig a channel for the salmon to swim down to the sea. That was all he had to do. He began to dig. The wet sand was heavy, but he would do it!

He dug and dug.

After a while, he stopped and looked to see how far he had gone. He had not gone very far at all. He kept on digging.

His mother called him for supper. He couldn't go because he hadn't finished yet.

The salmon was lying quietly now in the shallow water, waiting.

The sun dipped low in the sky and the air became cool. Simon's hands were red and he was getting a blister, but he kept on digging.

At last, just when he thought he couldn't lift another shovelful of sand, he looked up. There he was at the pool.

The channel was finished.

Cold sea water flowed into it. When the salmon felt the freshness of the sea, it began to move again. Its nose found the opening to the channel. Slowly, slowly the salmon began to swim down it, down to the sea.

Simon watched his shining salmon. Down, down, down the channel it swam. At last it reached the sea.

It dived deep into the cool green water. Then, gleaming in the last rays of the setting sun, it gave a great leap into the air.

It seemed to Simon that the salmon flicked its tail as if to say "thank you" before it disappeared beneath the waves.

"Good-bye, Sukai," called Simon.

The salmon was free at last.

Soon it would be in the deep, secret places of the sea.

Now the sun had set and a chilly wind was starting to blow. Simon's hands were sore and his feet were cold, but he felt warm inside, and happy. He picked up his fishing pole and his shovel and started for home.

And he knew, as he got near his house, that it would be bright and cheery inside because lamplight shone golden through the windows.

And he knew that it would be nice and warm, because he could see smoke curling out of the chimney.

And he knew that something good was cooking for supper because he could smell a delicious smell.

And Simon thought, as he opened the door, that maybe he would go fishing again tomorrow, after all.

But not for a salmon.

Questions

1. How did a salmon get into Simon's clam hole?

2. How did Simon feel as he watched the salmon swim down the channel?

3. What do you think Simon will do if he catches a fish?

4. If you had been Simon, how would you have tried to save the salmon?

Applying Reading Skills
Draw Conclusions

Read each conclusion below. Then write two or three sentences that give information to support the conclusion.

1. Simon wanted to catch a salmon more than anything else in the world.

2. Simon realized that he didn't want to hold on to the most beautiful fish in the world.

3. Simon was determined that the salmon should live.

4. Simon would never again fish for a salmon.

IS THAT YOUR OOMIAK?

When the boy in the story "A Salmon for Simon" tried to save the salmon, he called him *Sukai*. *Sukai* is the Eskimo word for salmon. It means "king of the fishes." *Sukai* might be a new word for you, but you already know some Eskimo words. Match these words with their meanings:

parka   a light, canvas canoe
kayak   house built of ice or snow
igloo   a warm winter coat

Here are some other Eskimo words that might not be as familiar to you:

mukluks   sealskin boots
oomiak   a large boat made of walrus skin
ulo   a curved knife
eskultea   school teacher

Now see if you can translate the underlined words in the sentences below.

1. When you go fishing for <u>sukai</u>, don't forget your <u>mukluks</u> and <u>parka</u>. Did you leave your <u>ulo</u> in the <u>oomiak</u>?
2. The <u>school teacher</u>, in her <u>warm coat</u> and <u>sealskin boots</u> climbed into the <u>canvas canoe</u>.

MY ISLAND GRANDMA

Kathryn Lasky

Simon knew the ways of the fish and birds that lived near his island. Abbey, the girl in this story, lives in the city. In the summer she visits her grandmother on an island. Together, they discover the plants, animals, and even some magic about living an island life.

I have a grandmother who swims in dark sea pools. She takes me with her early in the morning.

She has strong hands that hold me tight and safe in the cool deep water while I learn to swim.

Today she held me with two hands and I kicked my feet. Tomorrow when she holds me with one hand I will almost float.

And the next day she will hold me with just her finger and I WILL float.

The day after that no hands, no fingers, and I will swim away!

Grandma's hands are strong from taking down the big shutters every June from her cabin windows, and from digging the summer garden, and pumping buckets full of cold water at the well, and from carrying logs for the wood-burning stove.

It's very different on an island and we live there all summer long.

In June, after my dad closes up his classroom and my mom finishes painting winter stuff and packs her paintbox full of summer colors, we drive away from the city. We drive all through the night and day until we come to the ocean, where we leave our car behind and ride on a ferryboat to the island.

Grandma and her dog, Shadow, are already here, waiting with a wheelbarrow to carry our suitcases to our cabin.

After swimming in the morning we sit on a million-year-old rock and wrap ourselves up in big towels and we talk about things.

On our way home Grandma picks sea herbs that grow along the shore to make salad and sometimes she gathers periwinkles, little sea snails that live on rocks, to make soup.

I hate them both.

But I love to eat the blueberries we pick in the afternoon. When we pick the berries I pretend that I am a little bear, just like the story Grandma read to me, and that she is the mother bear. I growl and do bear things. I snap at her with my lips pulled over my teeth so it won't hurt. That's how baby bears get their mothers' attention.

One time on our way back from picking blueberries, Grandma called to me very softly, "Come over here, Abbey, and look at this."

I knew from her whispery voice that I should walk very quietly. So I tiptoed and when I got to where Grandma was standing, I saw a nest of dried grass at her feet. In the nest were three eggs—brown and gray with little speckles all over them.

One egg was jiggling just as if there were excited little feelings all closed up inside.

Then the egg bumped and rolled over showing a big bloody gash.

"Did it hurt itself?" I asked.

"No," Grandma said, "that's the blood that comes with new life."

Inside the bloody gash I could see a small beak, tinier than my little fingernail, pecking its way out of the egg.

Grandma said we had to go and pointed to the mother duck flying above. "She's angry that we're even near."

"But I want to stay! I really want to see this baby duck get born!"

"Absolutely not, Abbey. When you're getting born you need to be left with your own kind. People with people, ducks with ducks."

But I wanted to stay so badly. I really did.

Sometimes we go sailing, Grandma and Shadow and me. We sail in a little boat called *Memory*. It's painted white with a bright green stripe and Grandma's the skipper. She steers with the tiller and I hold the ropes for the sail and pull them at important times.

When we are sailing in *Memory* and there are lots of big clouds in the sky we tell cloud stories.

We look up in the sky and find special shapes in the clouds.

Once I said, "Look, Grandma! Remember the shark Daddy told us about? There it is swimming in the sky chasing the baby seal. It won't catch it this time because there's a cloud cave—see it? And it's just big enough for the seal pup to hide it."

Grandma says my stories are scary. She tells cloud stories about lambs and camels and sometimes disobedient children who do not eat their vegetables. And I always say, "Please, Grandma, no vegetable stories allowed. Just stories about plain bad children."

We make things on rainy days. We make moss gardens in old pie tins. We fill the pie tin with dirt and cover the dirt with thick green moss. Then we stick in the smallest plants. And if you look at the moss garden for a while it becomes a tiny world with little green mountains and little trees and valleys.

Sometimes we make moon cookies and star cookies and put silver sprinkles on them.

Grandma made me a special sleeping bag for when I spend the night. On the inside the sleeping bag is dark blue with pink and lavender flowers. It's just like sleeping in a flower cave with flowers growing everywhere— out of the ceiling, out of the walls, out of the floor.

I love to shine my flashlight in the flower cave in the middle of the night. I crawl way down to the foot of the bag where it is so dark you can breathe the blackness and then I press the flashlight button and suddenly there are a million flowers jumping and hopping all over.

And sometimes when I am sound asleep Grandma comes over to my sleeping bag and whispers in her night voice, "Abbey, Abbey, wake up and come with me outside. There's something special in the sky."

I get up and we both tiptoe in our nighties and we stand barefoot in the wet grass and the night wind blows. We look up at the starry sky and Grandma says, "Look, there's Lyra and Cygnus and Sagittarius and Capricorn." I say, "Speak English!" And she laughs her soft night laugh and says, "There's the Magic Harp, the Swan, the Archer, and the Sea Goat." And I look up and try to find the star pictures in the sky.

At the end of the summer Grandma closes up the island cabin. She puts shutters on all the windows and locks the door and we all go back to the city.

All winter long even though she wears shoes that make her taller and rides subways, I know that she is really my Island Grandma. She swims in dark sea pools, makes cloud stories and star pictures and flower caves and moon cookies.

She sails in her boat called *Memory* and she steers and I pull on the ropes at important times.

Questions

1. What are three things Abbey and her grandmother do together on the island?
2. How are cloud stories and star pictures alike?
3. What kind of a person do you think Abbey's grandmother is?
4. Describe some of the things you see and do outdoors in summer.

Applying Reading Skills
Character's Motives or Feelings

Use complete sentences to answer the questions below.

1. Why did Abbey's grandmother say that they couldn't stay to watch the baby duck get born?
2. How did Abbey feel when her grandmother made them leave before the duck was born?
3. How did Abbey feel about her grandmother's cloud stories?
4. Why did Abbey think of her grandmother as her Island Grandma even in the winter in the city?

SKILLS activity

CHARACTERS' MOTIVES OR FEELINGS

As you read a story carefully, you are able to understand more than just the words. You are able to understand the people in the story, too. The people in a story are the **characters.** Characters have reasons for acting the way they do. These reasons are called **motives.** Characters also have **feelings.** The way an author describes a character's motives and feelings helps us know the people we read about.

ACTIVITY Read the following stories. Then answer the questions about the characters' motives and feelings. Write your answers on your paper.

> Simon tried to catch a salmon all summer. Finally one day a bird dropped a live salmon in front of Simon. At last he would have a salmon to bring home! But when he looked at the beautiful fish, Simon felt sorry for it. He wanted to help it get back to the river.

What were Simon's motives for saving the fish?

a. It would be easier to catch in the water.
b. The fish was beautiful and he felt sorry for it.
c. The fish belonged to the bird.

How did Simon feel when the fish first dropped at his feet?

a. excited that he finally had a salmon
b. angry that a bird had dropped the fish
c. scared that the fish would bite him

Abbey's grandma teaches her lots of interesting things about nature. One day Grandma showed Abbey a nest with three eggs in it. One of the eggs was jiggling. A little beak was pecking out of it. Grandma pointed to a mother duck who was flying above. She explained that the duck was angry that people were near her babies. Abbey wanted to stay, but Grandma said they must leave the ducks.

What was Grandma's motive for showing Abbey the nest?

a. She wanted to make the mother duck angry.
b. She wanted to teach Abbey about nature.
c. She wanted to take the eggs home.

How did Grandma feel about the mother duck?

a. She was concerned that the duck was angry.
b. She was angry that the mother duck had left her nest.
c. She was sad that the duck didn't like Abbey.

BEAR MOUSE

Berniece Freschet
Illustrated by Donald Carrick

The life of an animal in the wild is full of adventure and also danger. The mouse in this story likes the safety and warmth of her nest. In order to survive and feed her young, she must use all her senses. Read to see how she faces the danger of the winter woods.

The snow was deep. A quilt of white
covered the meadow. It piled high against a
stone wall. Branches on the pine and birch bent
low.

Under the soft quilt, a meadow mouse,
shaggy as a little bear, ran down a snow tunnel.
Her path crossed another. She quickly turned,
following along the new mouse-trail.

There were many of these snowy tunnels
rambling through the meadow—a network of
trails that crossed and crossed again. They were
worn smooth by the constant running of tiny
mouse-feet.

Suddenly the little mouse stopped. She sat
up on her hind legs. She sat very still. Every
muscle in her small body was tense.

She had many enemies to look out for! What had she heard? A gray squirrel. . . . Or the soft, padded paws of a weasel overhead? The red fox slinking near? Or did she sense that the weasel and the bobcat were out on the hunt for a dinner of mouse, watching for the smallest telltale movement in the snow.

Her small ears, almost hidden under her coarse fur, listened for the smallest sound. She flicked an ear, brushing it against the tunnel wall.

She heard the musical tinkling of snow-crystals falling. Then all was quiet. Soon she hurried on, down the trail.

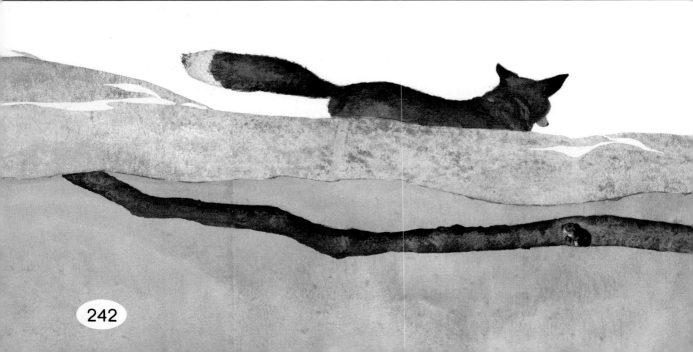

Another meadow mouse ran toward her. For a minute they stopped, their noses twitching . . . touching. They pushed past each other. Then off they ran in opposite directions, each intent on getting to somewhere.

A minute later the mouse pushed into an opening. Down she went to her nest in a tangle of twisted roots.

It was a good place, cozy and warm. In the middle of the nest, close together on a soft bed of dry grasses, lay four tiny mouse-babies. They smelled their mother's nearness. They squeaked their hunger. The tiny mice wanted their dinner. But there was little milk for the week-old babies.

During her last hunt, the meadow mouse had found only one dried hazelnut to eat. This was not enough food to make the milk to feed her hungry young.

Gently the mother mouse pushed her nose into the soft mound of fur. Her pink tongue licked each tiny mouse-baby. She chirruped soft sounds of comfort.

But the mouse knew she could not stay long. She must find something more to eat.

In jerky movements, she circled her babies. Then with one last quick turn, she left the nest, hurrying off down a snow tunnel. She moved into a trail that led upward. Soon she popped her head out of the snow.

She looked around. Her black, shiny eyes watched for signs of danger. All seemed safe. The little mouse came out of her tunnel. She ran to the foot of an old pine tree.

Sunlight sparkled on the white snow. There was a sudden flash of red as a cardinal flew out of the tree and swooped away across the meadow.

The mouse sat up, and with her front paws, she carefully cleaned the snow from her coat of fur. She looked different from most other kinds of mice.

Instead of a narrow pointed head, her head was round. Instead of a sleek, smooth body, hers was chunky. She had small ears and a hairy tail. Her legs were short. Her long, dark-brown hair made her legs seem even shorter. Because of her shaggy coat of fur, she looked like a "bear mouse."

The little meadow mouse was very hungry.

In the summer, when food was plentiful, she liked to eat seeds, roots, and berries. Her favorite food was sweet clover, and tender plants of alfalfa. But now the snow was deep and food was hard to find. Winter had come early this year. The mouse's storehouse of seeds was already gone.

She stuck her nose into a crack in the tree. She was looking for a bite of something—a weed seed, or maybe a dry tuft of moss. But she found nothing. She often visited the old pine tree. She had long ago picked it clean of every seed, every nut, every dry blade of grass.

High above in the blue sky, a hawk flew over the meadow. He swooped down. The black shadow of his wings skimmed across the white snow.

Quietly, nearer he flew.

The meadow mouse sat very still.

She sensed danger. The hawk dipped low. Sharp talons opened wide.

With a squeak, the mouse dived into the snow. She ran down a tunnel. Soon she stopped and crouched against the snow-path to rest.

She listened. Except for the wild beating of her heart, all was still.

When her fear passed, she hurried on. She came to a path that led up to the pond. Maybe she would find something to eat there. Up she climbed.

Turtle Pond was frozen over. Winter's quiet had come to the pond. The songbirds were gone. Many creatures were in hibernation, sleeping away the long, cold months.

The duck family who made their home here in the summer had flown to a warmer land. And the playful otters had long ago left for the big river.

The old bullfrog, the water snake, and the turtles were asleep. They were burrowed deep in the mud at the bottom of the pond.

Only the bigmouth bass and a few water creatures still swam under their roof of ice.

At the edge of the pond the mouse hunted for a snail. She looked for a water bug that might be caught in the snow. But the sparrows had already found and snapped up the trapped insects. There were no snails here, only two dry shells.

The mouse's stomach felt very empty. She licked at the snow. She darted under an alder bush and looked for an extra leaf or two that might still be hanging there. But the bush was bare, eaten clean by the deer. There was something else though. . . .

A cocoon hanging from a stem. Food!

Quickly the mouse ran up the stem. Holding the cocoon in her front paws, she ate it all. When she was finished, she ran under the low-hanging branches of a small spruce tree. Here she sat, cleaning her whiskers.

She felt better now, but she was still hungry. Soon out she dashed, running for the stone wall at the side of the meadow. She left behind her a trail of footprints in the soft snow.

The sun was low in the sky. The mouse would have to return to her babies soon. But first she needed more to eat. She had to find food to make milk for her young, or they would starve.

Overhead the cardinal flashed by. Something dropped from his bill. A red holly berry lay in the snow. The mouse hurried toward it. It was dangerous for her to be out in the open. But hunger made the mouse forget caution. She picked up the berry and began to eat it.

High in the old pine tree, a snowy owl looked out across the still, white meadow. He spread his great wings and sailed up and up.

"Whooo-whoo-whoo-" he called softly.

The little mouse heard the hunting cry of the owl. She darted for the safety of the stone wall. She crouched, waiting. Her small body shook with fear and hunger.

A snowshoe rabbit crouched near—one long ear bending forward. Quickly, in zigzagging leaps he ran away, hurrying for safe cover in the blackberry bushes.

For a while the mouse stayed close to the stone wall. But now she was more and more troubled. She had been away from her nest for too long. Even though she had not found food, she must return to her babies. The little mouse started across the meadow.

Suddenly she stopped. A strange, wild scent filled the air. The little mouse stood high. She looked around. She turned her head to one side and then to the other. Her ears twisted this way and that. She listened for the smallest sound. She sniffed the air.

At the edge of the meadow, a bobcat slunk low. He crept forward, toward the mouse.

Slowly, nearer and nearer crept the bobcat.

Now he was close enough.
He pounced!

The mouse leaped to one side. Again the bobcat sprang! The mouse dodged to the other side.

Twisting and turning, the little mouse raced for the safety of the stone wall. The cat was at her heels. She was almost to the wall. With a great bound, the bobcat leaped forward—

The mouse felt sharp claws rake her fur. End over end, she somersaulted across the snow.

In a last, desperate leap, the mouse sprang for the wall. She squeezed herself into a crack between the stones.

The cat pushed a paw inside. His sharp claws stretched toward the mouse, but he could not reach her. The little mouse was safe.

With an angry snarl the bobcat turned and trotted away to look for his supper at the pond.

Her close escape and her hunger had worn out the mouse. Her strength was almost gone. She was too weak now to return to her nest and her young.

She lay huddled against a rock, her small sides heaving. She rested. She ate a dry tuft of grass stuck between the stones. It was not much but it helped to fill her empty stomach. With her forepaws she pulled at the grass.

Suddenly, out of the crack between the stones, spilled acorns and weed seeds. It was a squirrel's forgotten storehouse of food.

Today the little mouse was lucky.

She ate and ate until her small stomach could not hold one seed more. Then she stuffed her cheeks full. Away she raced—back to her tunnels in the snow. She raced back to her nest and her family.

With tiny squeaks of delight, the mouse-babies welcomed their mother. She pulled them close.

When their stomachs were stretched tight with the warm milk, the mouse-babies snuggled into their mother's shaggy fur. Safe and warm in their cozy nest, the mouse-family went to sleep.

Questions

1. Why couldn't the mouse stay in the nest with her babies?

2. Will the mouse-babies be safe alone in the nest? Explain your answer.

3. Do you think the mouse will have as difficult a time finding food next winter? Why or why not?

4. Besides "bear mouse," what other name might you give to the mouse in the story?

Applying Reading Skills
Sequence of Events

Rewrite the following sentences in the correct order.

Safe and warm in their cozy nest, the mouse-family went to sleep.

The mouse sat up, and with her front paws, she carefully cleaned the snow from her coat of fur.

Holding the cocoon in her front paws, she ate it all.

The hawk dipped low.

In a last, desperate leap, the mouse sprang for the wall.

Suddenly, out of the crack between the stones, spilled acorns and weed seeds.

The Story of
Jumping Mouse

JOHN STEPTOE

Bear Mouse found food and went home to the safety of her nest. In this folk tale, a young mouse has hopes and dreams about traveling to a far-off land. He knows he will not be content until he gets there. In his travels, he finds ways to help others and discovers something about himself and the world.

Once there was a young mouse who lived in the brush near a great river. During the day he and the other mice hunted for food. At night they gathered to hear the old ones tell stories. The young mouse liked to hear about the desert beyond the river, and he got shivers from the stories about the dangerous shadows that lived in the sky. But his favorite was the tale of the far-off land.

The far-off land sounded so wonderful the young mouse began to dream about it. He knew he would never be content until he had been there. The old ones warned that the journey would be long and perilous, but the young mouse would not be swayed. He set off one morning before the sun had risen.

It was evening before he reached the edge of the brush. Before him was the river; on the other side was the desert. The young mouse peered into the deep water. "How will I ever get across?" he said in dismay.

"Don't you know how to swim?" called a gravelly voice.

The young mouse looked around and saw a small green frog.

"Hello," he said. "What is swim?"

"This is swimming," said the frog, and she jumped into the river.

"Oh," said the young mouse, "I don't think I can do that."

"Why do you need to cross the river?" asked the frog, hopping back up the bank.

"I want to go to the far-off land," said the young mouse. "It sounds too beautiful to live a lifetime and not see it."

"In that case, you need my help. I'm Magic Frog. Who are you?"

"I'm a mouse," said the young mouse.

Magic Frog laughed. "That's not a name. I'll give you a name that will help you on your journey. I name you Jumping Mouse."

As soon as Magic Frog said this, the young mouse felt a strange tingling in his hind legs. He hopped a small hop and, to his surprise, jumped twice as high as he'd ever jumped before. "Thank you," he said, admiring his powerful new legs.

"You're welcome," said Magic Frog. "Now step onto this leaf and we'll cross the river together."

When they were safely on the other side, Magic Frog said, "You will encounter hardship on your way, but don't despair. You will reach the far-off land if you keep hope alive within you."

Jumping Mouse set off at once, hopping quickly from bush to bush. The shadows circled above, but he avoided being seen. He ate berries when he could find them and slept only when he was exhausted. Days passed. Though he was able to travel quickly, he began to wonder if he'd ever reach the other side of the desert. He then came upon a stream that coursed through the dry land. Under a large berry bush he met a fat old mouse.

"What strange hind legs you have," said the fat mouse.

"They were a gift from Magic Frog when she named me," said Jumping Mouse proudly.

"Humpf," snorted the fat mouse. "What good are they?"

"They've helped me come this far across the desert, and with luck they'll carry me to the far-off land," said Jumping Mouse. "But now I'm very tired. May I rest here a while?"

"Indeed you may," said the fat mouse. "In fact, you can stay forever."

"Thank you, but I'll stay only until I'm rested. I've seen the far-off land in my dreams and I must be on my way as soon as I'm able."

"Dreams," said the fat mouse scornfully. "I used to have such dreams, but all I ever found was desert. Why go jumping about the desert when everything anyone needs is right here?"

Jumping Mouse tried to explain that it wasn't a question of need, but something he felt he had to do. But the fat mouse only snorted again. Finally Jumping Mouse dug a hole and curled up for the night.

The next day the fat mouse warned him to stay on this side of the stream. "A snake lives on the other side," he said. "But don't worry. He's afraid of water, so he'll never cross the stream."

Life was easy beneath the berry bush, and Jumping Mouse was soon rested and strong. He and the fat mouse ate and slept and then slept and ate. Then one morning, when he went to the stream for a drink, he caught sight of his reflection. He was almost as fat as the fat old mouse!

"It's time for me to go on," thought Jumping Mouse. "I didn't come all this way to settle down under a berry bush."

Just then he noticed that a branch had gotten caught in the narrow of the stream. It spanned the water like a bridge—now the snake could cross. Jumping Mouse hurried back to warn the fat mouse. But the mousehole was empty, and there was a strange smell in the air. Snake. Jumping Mouse was too late. "Poor old friend," he thought as he hurried away. "He lost hope of finding his dream and now his life is over."

Jumping Mouse traveled throughout the night, and the next morning he saw that he had reached a grassy plain. Exhausted, he hopped toward a large boulder where he could rest in safety. But as he got closer, he realized the boulder was an enormous, shaggy bison lying in the grass. Every once in a while it groaned.

Jumping Mouse shivered at the terrible sound. "Hello, great one," he said bravely. "I'm Jumping Mouse and I'm traveling to the far-off land. Why do you lie here as if you were dying?"

"Because I *am* dying," said the bison. "I drank from a poisoned stream, and it blinded me. I can't see to find tender grass to eat or sweet water to drink. I'll surely die."

Jumping Mouse was sad to see so wondrous a beast so helpless. "When I began my journey," he said, "Magic Frog gave me a name and strong legs to carry me to the far-off land. My magic is not as powerful as hers, but I'll do what I can to help you. I name you Eyes-of-a-Mouse."

As soon as he had spoken Jumping Mouse heard the bison snort with joy. He heard but he could no longer see, for he had given the bison his own sight.

"Thank you," said Eyes-of-a-Mouse. "You are small, but you have done a great thing. If you will hop along beneath me, the shadows of the sky won't see you, and I will guide you to the mountains."

Jumping Mouse did as he was told. He hopped to the rhythm of the bison's hooves, and in this way he reached the foot of the mountains.

"I am an animal of the plains, so I must stop here," said Eyes-of-a-Mouse. "How will you cross the mountains when you can't see?"

"There will be a way," said Jumping Mouse. "Hope is alive within me." He said good-bye to his friend; then he dug a hole and went to sleep.

The next morning Jumping Mouse woke to cool breezes that blew down from the mountain peaks. Cautiously he set out in the direction of the coolness. He had not gone far when he felt fur beneath his paws. He jumped back in alarm and sniffed the air. Wolf! He froze in terror, but when nothing happened he gathered up his courage and said, "Excuse me. I'm Jumping Mouse, and I'm traveling to the far-off land. Can you tell me the way?"

"I would if I could," said the wolf, "but a wolf finds his way with his nose, and mine will no longer smell for me."

"What happened?" asked Jumping Mouse.

"I was once a proud and lazy creature," replied the wolf. "I misused the gift of smell, and so I lost it. I have learned not to be proud, but without my nose to tell me where I am and where I am going, I cannot survive. I am lying here waiting for the end."

Jumping Mouse was saddened by the wolf's story. He told him about Magic Frog and Eyes-of-a-Mouse. "I have a little magic left," he said. "I'll be happy to help you. I name you Nose-of-a-Mouse."

The wolf howled for joy. Jumping Mouse could hear him sniffing the air, taking in the mountain fragrances. But Jumping Mouse could no longer smell the pine-scented breezes. He no longer had the use of his nose or his eyes. "You are but a small creature," said Nose-of-a-Mouse, "but you have given me a great gift. You must let me thank you. Come, hop along beneath me where the shadows of the sky won't see you. I will guide you through the mountains to the far-off land."

So Jumping Mouse hopped to the rhythm of the wolf's padding paws, and in this way he reached the far-off land.

"I am an animal of the mountains, so I must stop here," said Nose-of-a-Mouse. "How will you manage if you can no longer see or smell?"

"There will be a way," said Jumping Mouse. He then said good-bye to his friend and dug a hole and went to sleep.

The next morning Jumping Mouse woke up and crawled from his hole. "I am here," he said. "I feel the earth beneath my paws. I hear the wind rustling leaves on the trees. The sun warms my bones. All is not lost, but I'll never be as I was. How will I ever manage?" Then Jumping Mouse began to cry.

"Jumping Mouse," he heard a gravelly voice say.

"Magic Frog, is that you?" Jumping Mouse asked, swallowing his tears.

"Yes," said Magic Frog. "Don't cry, Jumping Mouse. Your unselfish spirit has brought you great hardship, but it is that same spirit of hope and compassion that has brought you to the far-off land."

"You have nothing to fear, Jumping Mouse."

"Jump high, Jumping Mouse," commanded Magic Frog.

Jumping Mouse did as he was told and jumped as high as he could. Then he felt the air lifting him higher still into the sky. He stretched out his paws in the sun and felt strangely powerful. To his joy he began to see the wondrous beauty of the world above and below and to smell the scent of earth and sky and living things.

"Jumping Mouse," he heard Magic Frog call. "I give you a new name."

"You are now called Eagle, and you will live in the far-off land forever."

Questions

1. What did Magic Frog give Jumping Mouse?
2. How was the fat mouse different from Jumping Mouse?
3. Why do you think Magic Frog turned Jumping Mouse into an eagle instead of just giving him back his senses?
4. If you could be an animal, what animal would you be? Why?

Applying Reading Skills
Sequence of Events

Rewrite the following sentences in the correct order.

Jumping Mouse met a fat old mouse.

A young mouse heard a tale of the far-off land.

Jumping Mouse met an enormous shaggy bison.

The young mouse met Magic Frog.

Jumping Mouse became an eagle who could live in the far-off land forever.

Jumping Mouse was saddened by the wolf's story.

John Steptoe

John Steptoe "connects" with the world through his art.

John Steptoe grew up in the same neighborhood in Brooklyn, New York, where he lives today with his own family. But in his life, as in his art, he has shown a desire to try new things and change. He wrote and illustrated his first book, *Stevie*, when he was only seventeen. Most of Steptoe's books come out of his experience of growing up in a black neighborhood. Yet characters like Stevie appeal to everyone.

"I want to tell stories that communicate how I see things," Steptoe says. "And I like to tell stories that I think will be read out loud. I have always liked to listen to storytellers. I heard the story of Jumping Mouse years ago. It has surfaced in my memory many times. To me "Jumping Mouse" is a story about hanging in there when the going gets tough and not giving up hope. When I retold it, I stressed what the story really meant to me."

More to Read   *Stevie, Train Ride*

BIRDS & BEARS IN WINTER

Franklyn M. Branley

The long winter's cold presents problems for many animals. Birds can't burrow under the ground as mice can. Bears are too big to live long on the small bits of food they might find in the snow. Read to find out how some animals— small birds and big bears—survive in the winter.

You don't see many birds in winter. Most have left your area. Those that stay are not as active. Activity uses energy that is needed to keep warm.

The worst problems for birds in winter are getting enough heat and holding on to the heat once it is made. These are problems for all birds. But it is especially true for very small ones. They cannot find enough food. The weather stays so cold for so long that they cannot eat enough to keep alive. But birds have many ways of fighting the cold.

You shiver to keep warm. The heat that you make is made mostly in your muscles. The muscles make more heat when they are active.

So one way of keeping warm is to move about, use your muscles. Another way is to shiver. When your body needs heat, the muscles tighten and loosen quickly. They become active. Just as you shiver to keep warm, so do birds.

When it's cold, temperatures go down and down. When it's 10° below zero and the wind is blowing 30 miles an hour, the temperature feels like 63° below zero. The wind makes air seem even colder. Yet birds survive. They keep alive by eating, and by shivering. They shiver without stopping. They just perch and shiver. They make as much heat as possible. They stay still so they use as little as possible. Shivering helps a bird to make four or five times more heat than it would make if it were not shivering. The only times birds leave a perch is to look for more food. Shivering is only one way that birds keep alive during very cold weather.

Another way that birds reduce the amount of heat they need is by lowering their body temperature. You and I are not able to do this. Humans need to keep their body temperature at 98.6°, or very close to it. When a bird is active, its body temperature is 104°, higher than your temperature. But when a bird rests or sleeps its body temperature drops. The bird can survive even when its temperature has dropped some 20 degrees, to about 84°. Birds can store up only a small amount of food. Their bodies aren't large enough to hold much. So one way of stretching the amount of food is to lower the body temperature. Lower temperatures mean that food is used more slowly. Birds can "turn up the thermostat" in the morning. In a few minutes their body temperature is once more at 104°. Then the bird becomes active.

Birds shiver to make more heat. They drop their temperature so less heat is needed. But they must still save whatever heat they have. One way they do this is by increasing their insulation. They grow more feathers. Many of the feathers they grow are the down that grows under the large outer feathers. This is one of the best of all insulators. Jackets filled with down are light, but very warm. A down-filled blanket, or comforter, makes you feel warm in bed because it is light. It keeps you from losing heat. The down traps air. A down-covered bird loses very little heat. As the temperature drops, birds fluff their feathers. They trap greater amounts of air among the down feathers. They hunch on a limb and stay still. This way they can keep quite warm even when temperatures may be well below zero.

Often you can't see the birds unless you look for them. They don't perch out in the open. Birds look for a place that protects them from the wind and storms. A favorite perch is on the inside branches of pine trees. There the needles cover them. The wind doesn't strike them.

When there is not much snow, birds can find food such as seeds. But those that eat insects, like woodpeckers, have a hard time. And all birds must look when the ground is snow covered. If you happen to live in the country, it's a good idea to put out seeds for the birds. You can put out pieces of fat for the insect eaters. That's especially true when the temperature is low. Birds cannot spend a lot of energy looking for food. If they can get food quickly, as they can at a feeder, they can keep warmer. Also, if there is a lot of food, the birds can eat their fill. Then they will have enough food inside them to last several hours.

Many birds die during cold weather. Many others live because they fluff their feathers. They drop their body temperature and shiver. They are lucky enough to find lots of food. They know how to keep warm, even when it is very cold. And so do many animals, especially black bears.

Black bears escape winter's cold as much as they can. In winter they sleep a long time. They nestle deep inside a small cave or a hollow tree. Even though the temperature may drop to 30° or 40° below zero, a bear keeps warm.

As soon as spring brings a new growth of bushes and berries, bears start feeding. They eat and eat. All through the spring and summer their feeding goes on. The bears build themselves up. They store food and fats that they will need in the fall when they start their long sleep. As the days grow shorter, and the temperature begins to fall, bears hunt for a sleeping place. It may be a shallow cave, or a deep crack between rocks. Some bears end up sleeping in hollow logs. Logs seem to be bears' favorite places. Bears seem to choose small spaces. They can keep warmer in a cave that's just large enough to hold them than in a larger cave. They often line their sleeping place with leaves and dried grass. No food is stored in the cave. All through their winter naps, bears will not eat. Often they will sleep for 7 months, moving only now and then. During that time they neither eat nor drink.

Very often the females will give birth to cubs sometime in January. The cubs do not hibernate, but they sleep a lot. About all they do is nurse and sleep.

Normally a bear's body temperature is about 100°. During its winter sleep this temperature drops only about 12 degrees. Bears use the fat stored in their bodies to keep the temperature high enough. It's a wonder that bears can do this, even when the temperature may be way below zero.

They are able to keep warm for reasons you already know about. They are not active, so just about all their energy goes toward keeping warm. Even their heart rate goes way down. When a bear is walking about and feeding, its heart beats between 50 and 90 times. During the long winter sleep, the heart often beats only 8 times a minute. That is just enough to keep the blood circulating. If a bear is roused a bit, it might lift its head and look around in a sleepy kind of way. Then the heart rate would increase a little. And the heart must beat faster when the bear gives birth to her cubs.

Because of the slowdown in body needs, bears can make enough heat to keep warm. But once the heat is made, it must be saved. In other words, bears must be well insulated. It helps that their sleeping places are lined with leaves and grass. Also, as winter nears, new hair grows. The hair comes in thick and full. When the bear fluffs it up, air is trapped between the hairs. It is also trapped between the outside hair and the bear's skin.

Another way bears save heat is to curl up. They make themselves into a ball, just as you do when you're cold. They stick their noses into their bellies. Then they stay that way. Less body surface exposed to the air means more heat.

Black bears don't try to fight winter's weather. They curl up and wait until spring brings new branches, leaves, and berries.

People cannot get away from winter so easily. They can't snuggle for a winter nap that covers several months. However, people have learned how to endure winter by building tight houses. These houses hold the heat they put into them. They have learned to eat an energy-giving diet. And people also wear clothing that slows the loss of body heat.

Questions

1. What are three things birds do to keep warm?

2. Why don't black bears need to fight winter's weather?

3. Do you think birds or bears have a harder time surviving in winter? Explain your answer.

4. Compare the ways people and animals keep warm in winter.

Applying Reading Skills
Main Idea

Read the following paragraph from "Birds and Bears in Winter." Then write the main idea of the paragraph in your own words.

Often you can't see the birds unless you look for them. They don't perch out in the open. Birds look for a place that protects them from the wind and storm. A favorite perch is on the inside branch of pine trees. There the needles cover them. The wind doesn't strike them.

Hungry Morning

In December I remember
In the rain and frosty snow
   hungry cardinals,
   hungry blue jays,
   hungry sparrows: Here I go.
Here's a piece of toast I've saved you
From my breakfast, warm and good,
   hurry cardinals,
   hurry blue jays,
   hurry sparrows: Here's your food.

Myra Cohn Livingston

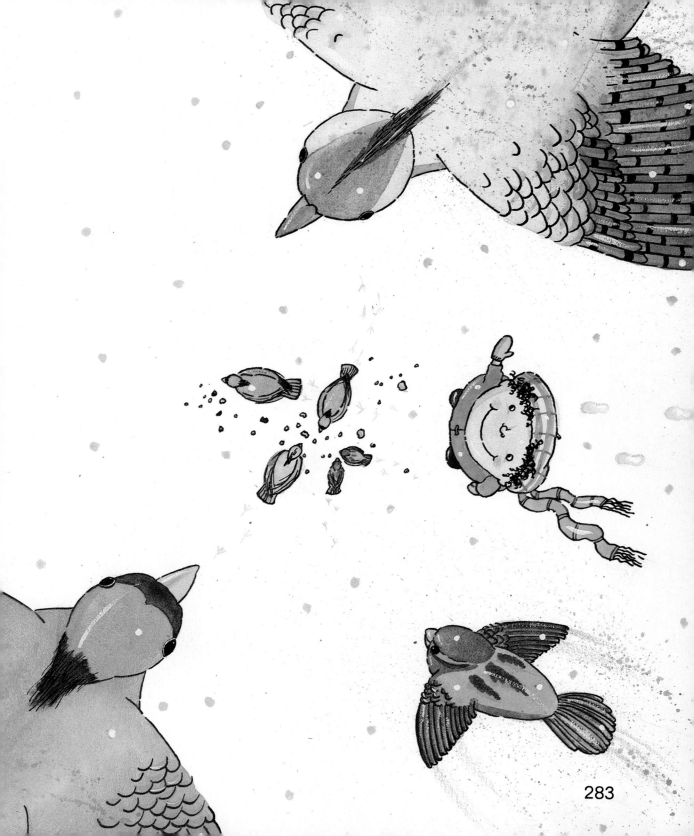

283

SKILLS activity

HOMOGRAPHS

Some words look alike because they are spelled alike. But these words may not sound alike or have the same meaning. You have to read how the word is used in a sentence. Then you will know how to say the word, and you will know which meaning of the word to use. Here is an example:

Bears <u>live</u> in caves through the winter.
We caught a <u>live</u> mouse.

In the first sentence, *live* means "to make one's home." In the second sentence, *live* means "having life, not dead." The words *live* and *live* are **homographs.** They are spelled alike, but they do not sound alike and they have different meanings.

ACTIVITY Read each set of word meanings. Then read each numbered sentence. Choose the right meaning for each underlined word. Write that meaning on your paper.

To **wind** is to wrap something in a circle.
The **wind** is fast moving air.

1. Wind up the kite string on the stick.
2. The wind blew through the trees.

To **record** is to put sound onto a disk or tape.
A **record** is a disk that makes sound when it is played on a machine.

1. I have a record of bird songs.
2. Let's record our class song.

To be **close** is to be very near something.
To **close** is to shut something.

1. Bear cubs stay close to their mothers.
2. People close their doors and windows in winter.

A **desert** is a very dry land with few plants.
To **desert** is to go away and leave someone or something.

1. A mother mouse would never desert her babies.
2. Mice and snakes are two animals that live in the desert.

THE GRIZZLY BEAR WITH THE GOLDEN EARS

Jean Craighead George

In the summer, the brown grizzly bears of
Alaska fish salmon out of the river. Golden Ears
is one of these bears who makes life difficult
for animals and people. What sad lesson must
Golden Ears learn?

The people of the North called her Golden Ears. She had round blond ears that set her apart from all other bears. She was a brown grizzly bear of Alaska.

Golden Ears lived in the ice-bitten forest of Katmai. In the summer she and the other bears of the forest fished for salmon in the Brooks River. In autumn they wandered the mountains eating blueberries and cranberries. In the winter when ice storms crackled, they slept under the roots of the spruce trees in the foothills of the rugged Aleutian Mountains.

Golden Ears was three years old.

One sunny noon in June she brought her little golden-eared cub to meet the bears of the Brooks River. They were gathered on the riverbank.

The bears stepped back and lowered their heads. A mother bear with a cub is both queen and king. She is the most adored bear of all bears. Even Ursus stepped back. He was a one-thousand-pound male grizzly. He had killed a little cub. Some male bears do this when they find one alone and unguarded.

Below Brooks Falls the red salmon gathered by the thousands to leap up the waterfall. The fish leave the Pacific Ocean. They swim up the rivers to the same streams where they were born.

There in the shallows under the starflowers, the salmon lay their eggs and die. As they swim home they are eaten by wolves, eagles, and gulls. Along the Brooks River, the people fish for them. The ranger fishes. So do the rollicking, diving, wonderful brown grizzly bears.

Golden Ears splashed into the churning water. She snapped at a fish and missed. Golden Ears swatted another fish and missed.

In a pool nearby, Kasvik, her friend, put her head under the water. She saw a salmon, snapped her jaws and caught it. She carried it up on the shore. Golden Ears wanted that fish. She was boss bear. So she lunged at Kasvik, bluffing her, as bears do. Kasvik dropped the salmon and ran. Golden Ears sat down by her golden-eared cub. She cleaned the bones from the fish and daintily ate it.

The next day she bluffed Kuka and took his fish. And the following day she pounced at her sister and took her fish. Feeling very sure of herself, she walked up to Ursus.

"Yarl," she growled. The enormous grizzly dropped his fish and backed away.

Golden Ears did not bother to fish. She just bluffed all the bears on the Brooks River. She ate until she was full.

Then she romped with her cub in the aspen grove. They watched the eaglets in their nest.

One summer afternoon when the sun flashed on the river, Golden Ears came upon a fisherman. He was pulling a huge fish out of a pool.

She hesitated, because she was afraid of people; but she was boss bear. She charged the fisherman. He dropped rod, reel, bait, and lunch. He ran in terror back to fish camp to report the terrible bear with the golden ears.

Out in the river, Golden Ears tore open the lunch bag. She found ham sandwiches and fruit. She carried them back to the aspen grove, and she and her cub ate them.

Ursus stalked the forest behind them.

When the winds of August blew, the salmon run slowed down. The bears of the Brooks River caught fewer and fewer fish. A young boy came to the waterfall and cast his line. He caught a big salmon and hauled it ashore.

Golden Ears rushed at the boy and growled. He dropped his rod, reel, fish, and lunch. Then he ran full speed to the ranger.

"A bear with golden ears almost ate me," he said. "So I dropped my fish and lunch, and ran."

"That is the last time *that* bear will bluff,"
said Karen the ranger. "I am going to give her a
shot to put her to sleep for a while." She picked
up the phone and called the forester. "Come in
your helicopter and get Golden Ears," she said.
"Put her and her cub in the net. Carry them
hundreds of miles away. Then let them go."
Then Karen asked the boy to lead her to
Golden Ears.

Golden Ears was eating sandwiches in the aspen grove. Ursus was nearby. Presently he lumbered past them and dove into the river. He belly flopped on a salmon. Golden Ears got to her feet. She challenged Ursus. He ran up the bank, and the fish was hers. When she had cleaned and eaten the fish she climbed back to her cub.

He was gone.

She looked for him in the aspen grove. She searched the meadow, ran through the flowers. She called and roared in sadness and fear.

She thundered into the forest out of sight of the ranger. She knocked down trees. She uprooted ferns and moss as she hunted for her cub. Then she stood up. Walking on two feet, she sniffed and called. No little cub answered.

All night Golden Ears searched the riverbank. She woofed and cried and suffered. Just before the misty morning dawned, she lowered her head. She moved miserably toward her den on the mountain.

The bears of the Brooks River stood still and listened.

"Woof," Golden Ears called (Where are you, little one?). "Woof. Woof."

A gray wolf howled. The eaglets called. Golden Ears gave up the hunt. She walked in silence.

"Wuf," came a small voice. A tree swayed. Golden Ears snapped up her head. She rose to her hind feet and stared. In the top of the spruce her golden-eared cub looked down at her.

Golden Ears whimpered and woofed as her cub backed into her arms. She flopped back on her haunches and hugged him. She licked, kissed, and loved him.

Then she got to her feet. Her cub close to her heels, she tramped down the mountain. She crossed the Brooks River, and jogged along the shore of Lake Naknek, around the rocky foot of Mount Katolinat and out across the marshland.

She passed a moose. She walked under clouds of swallows, and trotted for miles and miles to the shores of the Margot River.

On the riverbank she twitched her golden ears and watched hordes of salmon swim by. Then, with a loud ker-splash, she dove. She came up with a fish and never went back to the bears of the Brooks River.

Questions

1. How did Golden Ears get her fish?

2. Was Golden Ears really a danger to the fisherman and the boy? Why or why not?

3. Why do you think Golden Ears stopped bluffing at the end of the story?

4. Think about and then describe a time in real life when bluffing could get a person into trouble.

Applying Reading Skills
Draw Conclusions

Read each conclusion below. Then write two or three sentences that give information to support the conclusion.

1. Golden Ears tricked the other bears out of their fish.

2. Golden Ears only meant to scare other bears and people out of their fish.

3. Golden Ears began to fish for herself because she was so happy her cub had returned.

4. The ranger never had to send Golden Ears away, because she traveled a long way herself in search of her cub.

What's For Lunch?

Sally Tongren

Snails, wentletraps, mice, eagles, salmon, and grizzly bears are all animals found in North America. What about giant pandas, African elephants, and Atlas lions? They are not found in the wilds of North America.

The National Zoological Park in Washington, D.C., is a home for these and many other kinds of animals. As you read, think about how your needs and the needs of these animals are the same and different.

National
Zoological
Park

Smithsonian
Institution

It is morning at the National Zoological Park in Washington, D.C. It is feeding time for the lions and tigers before they go into their outdoor yards for the day. Keepers wheel carts along the walkway. The carts carry the day's food for the big cats.

In his cage the male Atlas lion stretches and walks near the wire fence. His food drops through the feeding chute. He is a beautiful animal. He has a great mane that covers his shoulders and chest. Once lions traveled the North African lands between the Mediterranean and the Atlas Mountains. They were the lions of legends and stories. The zoo's Atlas lions lie in the sun. Their fat golden paws are folded before them. But they can be as picky about their food as any house cat. Today, the lion puts his head down and sniffs at his meal. Then he turns away with a twitch of his tail.

The zoo is trying to give all its big cats a new kind of prepared diet. The Atlas lion will gladly eat raw horse meat or beef. But he will have no part of the new food. So the keepers are working out mixtures to win him over.

This story is about the feeding at only one zoo. Most other zoos feed their animals in the same way. Today's zoos are much different than they were thirty years ago. At one time, zoo curators were happy if they just kept animals alive for a time. They thought many kinds of animals were too delicate to survive in captivity. They did not try to breed them. Besides, there were many animals in the wild. If a zoo needed a new elephant or tiger, one could be caught. Care and feeding of zoo animals were far from scientific. Zoos were mainly places for fun.

Today, zoos don't just try to keep the animals alive. The aim is to have healthy animals with glossy coats or bright feathers.

The Atlas lion is one animal that is becoming extinct in the wild. Zoos hope that their lions will have cubs. Then the Atlas lion may not die out. Zoos are still fun. But the best ones try to help and learn about their animals.

One of the most important parts of animal health is good food. Nutrition is important for animals as well as for people. The National Zoo has a nutritionist who studies the things that animals eat. Bamboo and earthworms do not come with labels on them that tell what is in them. The nutritionist learns what the animals need to eat to be healthy.

Thirty years ago, all carnivores got raw meat. Carnivores are animals that eat other animals to live. All hoofed animals—like deer and elk—got hay. But we have learned more about animals and their differences. We have also learned that they need certain foods in just the right amounts. The planning and preparation of zoo food has become very important.

The day begins early at the zoo. At 5 A.M. even the birds are still asleep. But the lights shine in the Bird House kitchen as a keeper starts his or her work. Many used feeding pans wait by the sink to be cleaned.

Pans washed, the keeper starts to prepare the day's food. Apples, oranges, bananas, and kale wait for chopping. Cans of sweet potatoes and fruit are opened. Meat and fish are set out to defrost. By this time, the birds are beginning to wake up. The keeper goes on with his or her work as the sounds of the birds grow louder and louder.

The keeper has to chop some apples into small pieces. Other apples are minced. Kale goes through the mincing machine. It comes out looking like ground parsley. Oranges and bananas are cut up. Fish and meat are sliced.

Nectar mix is made to feed the birds. Nectar mix is a mix of water, honey, wheat germ oil or carrot oil. Oyster shells are ground to give the birds grit. Many birds, such as seed-eaters, need grit or gravel in their diets. Since they have no teeth, food is ground in their gizzards. There, grit helps grind the food.

Extra fruit is added for other animals. A mouse is added here, some seed there. Then the food pans are brought to the cages by the full team of keepers who have come by this time.

Preparing food for the Bird House is probably the hardest job in the zoo. But in the buildings where the reptiles, small mammals, and other animals are kept, the same kind of thing is going on.

The day begins about 6 A.M. at the commissary. The fresh food for the whole zoo is kept there. The kitchens in the animal houses haven't space to store lots of fresh food. Large tubs are filled with apples. One tub is for the Bird House. One is for the Reptile House. One is for the bears, and so on. There are also special orders. The apes and monkeys have a different vegetable every day. They have carrots, green beans, turnips, or onions. Meat for the cats, bears, and wolves is weighed out and mixed.

Each animal house orders food from the commissary every week. The food is sent every day. Meals have to be on time. Animals cannot wait for their food. Some birds and shrews can starve within a day if feeding is late.

The commissary is the main part of the zoo. Food for the animals is the most important job. If fish or fruit do not come on time, the commissary has to find other foods right away.

Food for the National Zoo costs hundreds of thousands of dollars each year. What does this buy? The list goes on for pages. For example, these foods are eaten each month:

Apples	3,500 pounds
Kale	2,500 pounds
Bananas	2,000 pounds
Corn on the cob	700 ears
Onions	100 pounds
Coconuts	50 nuts
Rib and shank bones	3,000 to 4,000 pounds
Fish	9,650 pounds
Adult mice	8,000 to 12,000 pounds
Rats	900
Crickets	150,000 to 175,000
Night crawlers	3,500

These are all fresh foods. There are many different canned and dried foods as well. These foods are used more and more. They are used mostly because they are balanced and complete diets. An animal that eats these foods can't pick through the pan and take only what it likes. Also, it is hard to mix small bits of food by hand and be sure that everything is balanced well. So more and more, the zoo's nutritionist is using prepared foods.

By noon at the National Zoo, most of the animals have been fed. There is time for the keepers to work at other jobs. One job is going out into nearby gardens to cut bamboo for the pandas. The giant pandas eat thirty or more pounds of bamboo a day. The zoo grows some bamboo, but most of it comes from kind neighbors.

The zoo buys its own insects to make meals for lizards, frogs, and salamanders.

By 4 P.M. the zoo day is winding down. Those animals that have afternoon feedings are eating happily. Foods for the next day are prepared, weighed, and measured. Then they are held in refrigerators and storerooms all around the zoo. It has been a busy day. Some late visitors watch the pandas eating their bamboo. They laugh at the monkeys. But few of them have any idea of the time and work and planning that lie behind the food that they see.

Questions

1. How do the keepers feed the lions at the zoo?

2. Why has nutrition become important at zoos?

3. Do you think zoos should completely replace fresh foods with prepared foods? Why or why not?

4. How are the needs of your home and this animal home alike and different?

Applying Reading Skills
Main Idea

Read the following paragraph from "What's For Lunch?" Then write the main idea of the paragraph in your own words.

Each animal house orders food from the commissary every week. The food is sent everyday. Meals have to be on time. Animals cannot wait for their food. Some birds and shrews can starve within a day if feeding is late.

DIGGING UP
DINOSAURS
by ALIKI

To learn about animals, you can watch them in the wild or in zoos. You can also learn about them in museums. Museums are the only place where you can see animals—such as dinosaurs—that lived long ago. But dinosaurs didn't start out inside museums. How did they get there? You're about to read of an unusual trip into the world of dinosaurs.

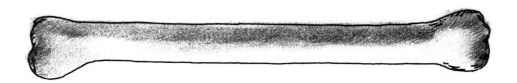

Have you ever seen dinosaur skeletons in a museum? I have. I visit them all the time. I went again yesterday.

I saw APATOSAURUS. I saw CORYTHOSAURUS. I saw IGUANODON and TRICERATOPS. I like to say their names.

STEGOSAURUS was just where I had left it. And TYRANNOSAURUS REX looked as fierce as ever. TYRANNOSAURUS used to scare me. I still can't believe how big it is. Just its head is almost twice my size.

I'm not afraid of dinosaurs anymore.
Sometimes I call them "you bag of bones" under
my breath. I can spend hours looking at them.
I used to wonder where they came from and
how they got into the museum. But now I know.

Dinosaurs lived millions of years ago. A few
of them were as small as birds, but most were
huge.

Some dinosaurs ate plants. Some dinosaurs
ate the meat of other dinosaurs, and some may
have eaten the eggs of other dinosaurs.

Dinosaurs lived everywhere. They lived on
every continent in the world. They lived in Asia,
Africa, North America, South America, Europe,
Australia, and Antarctica.

Then they died out. No one
knows for sure why they became
extinct. But they did. There
has not been a dinosaur
around for 65 million
years.

Until about 200 years ago, no one knew anything about dinosaurs. Then people began finding things in rock. They found large footprints. They found huge bones and strange teeth. People were finding fossils.

Fossils are a kind of diary of the past. They are the remains of plants and animals that died long ago. Instead of rotting or falling apart, the remains were preserved. They slowly turned to stone.

Fossil hunters found more and more big bones in different parts of the world. Scientists studied the fossils. They said the bones and teeth and footprints all belonged to a group of giant reptiles that lived on earth for millions of years. The giants were named DINOSAURIA, or TERRIBLE LIZARD.

What finds these were! People crowded into museums to see them. But the dinosaur bones didn't just get up and walk there. They had to be dug out of the ground slowly and patiently.

Even today, digging up dinosaurs is not an easy job. A team of experts must work together.

A paleontologist studies ancient plants and animals. A geologist knows the age of rocks and fossils. A draftsperson draws pictures of the fossils. Workers dig the fossil out of the rock. A photographer takes pictures of the find. Specialists prepare the fossil for the museum.

This is how fossil hunters work. First, they have to find a dinosaur. They search along riverbanks. They look in quarries. They climb up high cliffs. They go down into steep canyons.

PALEONTOLOGIST

A scientist who studies ancient plants and animals.

This skull belonged to a plant-eater named SCELIDOSAURUS.

With luck, someone spots a fossil bone coming out of the rock. The site is covered with a tent, and the work begins.

Sometimes the fossil is buried very deep. Then the rock around it has to be drilled or blasted. Tons of rubble are carted away. Scientists chip at the rock close to the fossil. They brush away the grit. They have to be very careful.

As soon as a bone is uncovered, it is brushed with shellac. The shellac helps hold the bone together, so it won't fall apart. Then the bone is numbered.

Sometimes a skeleton has to be cut apart so that it can be moved. The draftsperson draws each bone in its exact place. The photographer takes pictures. That way, there can be no mix-up later when someone tries to put the skeleton together.

When the bones are ready to be moved, they are carefully wrapped. Small bones are wrapped in tissue paper. Then they are put into boxes or sacks.

GEOLOGIST

A scientist who knows the age of rocks and fossils.

Large bones are left in the rock. They will be dug out later, in the museum. These fossils are covered with a plaster cast, just as a broken leg is.

Humm.

Each bone is then packed in straw. Then the bones are put in crates and taken to the museum.

At the museum, scientists unwrap the fossil. They finish digging it out of the rock. They study the bones.

They compare the bones to other dinosaur bones. They compare them to the bones of other animals. They try to figure out what size and shape the dinosaur was. They try to find out how the dinosaur stood and walked, and what it ate.

If there are enough bones, scientists are able to build a complete skeleton. A frame is made in the shape of the dinosaur. It supports the bones. The bones are wired together, one by one. They are held in place with pieces of metal. If any bones are missing, plastic or fiberglass ones are made to replace them. You can hardly tell the new bones from the old.

After many months the work is complete. The dinosaur skeleton looks just as it once did.

Until lately, only a few museums had dinosaurs. Then scientists learned to make copies of the skeletons. The copy is hard to make. It takes a long time. The original skeleton has to be taken completely apart, bone by bone. A mold is made for each bone.

The new pieces are made of fiberglass. A fiberglass dinosaur is just as scary as the original. But it is much stronger and lighter.

Now museums all over the world have dinosaur skeletons. And many people can spend hours looking at them, the way I do.

Questions

1. How did people find out about dinosaurs?

2. Why are the dinosaur bones so delicate and brittle?

3. Do you think it is a good idea to make fiberglass dinosaurs? Why or why not?

4. If you were on the team of experts digging up dinosaurs, which job would you like to have?

Applying Reading Skills
Sequence of Events

Rewrite the following sentences in the correct order.

Scientists begin to chip at the rock close to the fossil.

The bone is numbered.

Someone finds a fossil bone coming out of a rock.

The bone is taken to the museum.

The bone is uncovered and it is brushed with shellac.

The photographer takes pictures.

The site is covered with a tent.

The bones are wired together to make a skeleton.

The bones are wrapped and put into boxes.

LONG GONE

Don't waste your time in looking for
the long-extinct tyrannosaur,
because this ancient dinosaur
just can't be found here anymore.

This also goes for stegosaurus,
allosaurus, brontosaurus
and any other saur or saurus.
They all lived here long before us.

Jack Prelutsky

315

SKILLS activity

SEQUENCE OF EVENTS

When you read about something, it helps you understand the story if you know the order in which things happened in the story. That order is called the **sequence of events** in the story.

ACTIVITY A   Read the story. Then read each question. Write the correct answer on your paper.

> The day for zookeepers begins at 2 A.M. in the birdhouse. First they clean yesterday's feeding pans. Then they chop up fresh fruit. They defrost meat and fish. Then they grind oyster shells to give the birds grit. At last the food is ready to be brought to the birds.

1. What do the zookeepers do first?
   a. chop up fresh fruit
   b. grind oyster shells
   c. clean the feeding pans

2. When are the oyster shells ground?
   a. before the meat is defrosted
   b. after the meat is defrosted
   c. after the birds eat

3. What do the zookeepers do last?

    a. bring the food to the birds

    b. clean the next day's feeding pans

    c. chop the fruit

ACTIVITY B Read the story. Think about the order in which scientists put together dinosaur skeletons.

      Scientists search along riverbeds until they find some fossils. They drill and blast the rock around the bones. They uncover the bones and number them. Each bone is packed and taken to the museum. If there are enough bones, scientists are able to build a complete skeleton.

Write the sentences below on your paper. Write numbers 1 to 6 after the sentences to show in what order scientists do things.

Scientists pack the bones._____

Scientists drill and blast the rock._____

Scientists search for fossils._____

Scientists build a skeleton._____

Scientists uncover and number the bones._____

Scientists take the bones to the museum._____

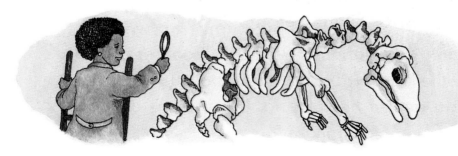

CAM JANSEN
AND THE
MYSTERY OF THE
DINOSAUR BONES
David A. Adler

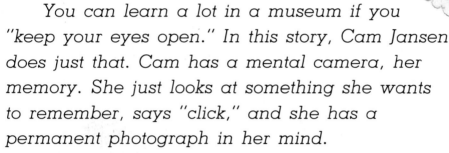

You can learn a lot in a museum if you "keep your eyes open." In this story, Cam Jansen does just that. Cam has a mental camera, her memory. She just looks at something she wants to remember, says "click," and she has a permanent photograph in her mind.

Cam and her class go to a museum. During the tour of the dinosaur exhibit, Cam notices that some bones are missing from the tail of the Coelophysis, one of the dinosaur fossils. Her friend Eric believes her, but no one else will— not the museum guards or even the museum director.

Eric and Cam are about to give up when they spot a mysterious milk truck. Soon they are hot on the trail of the missing dinosaur bones.

Cam got on her bicycle. "Come on," she said to Eric. "Let's follow the truck."

The streets were crowded with cars. It was after four o'clock, and many people were driving home from work. Cam stayed on the right-hand side of the street. Eric rode behind her. The milk truck was already a block ahead. Cam and Eric pedaled hard to catch up.

The milk truck made a right turn onto a side street. When Cam and Eric reached the corner, they signaled and turned. But they couldn't see the milk truck.

"We've lost it," Cam said.

"Maybe not. I think I see a truck parked in the driveway of one of the houses on the next block. Maybe it's the milk truck."

Eric led Cam to a small brick house with a white wooden fence around it. The milk truck was parked in the driveway. No one was sitting inside the truck.

"They must have gone into the house," Cam said. She leaned her bicycle against the fence. "You stay here and watch for them," she told Eric. "I'll look around in the back."

There was a high window on the side of the garage. As Cam walked past the window, she heard voices. She looked for something to stand on so she could see inside.

Someone tapped her on the back. It was Eric.

"I left the bicycles against the fence," he said. "I didn't want to wait out there alone."

Cam found an empty wooden milk box behind the house. She put the box right under the window, climbed up, and looked through.

There was a large table inside the garage. A few small bones and some larger ones were on the table. The milk box with the brown bag that they had seen the man put in the truck was there, too. A bag of plaster of Paris was on the floor near some boxes, and metal tubs and a wheelbarrow with a pickax and shovel in it.

Eric climbed up on the box.

"Look!" Eric said. "The three missing bones are on that table!"

Eric got off the box. He pulled on Cam's sleeve. "Get down," he said. "Let's go back now."

Cam didn't move. She kept looking through the window.

"We can call the museum," Eric said. "We can tell them we found their missing dinosaur bones."

"Someone is coming through the door," Cam said. "It's the Milkman."

Eric quickly climbed onto the box. Cam and Eric watched the Milkman take the brown bag out of the box.

"I wonder what could be in there," Eric whispered.

"It can't be a bone from the Coelophysis," Cam said quietly. "It's too big."

The Milkman tore open the side of the bag. There was something large and white inside. He took it out and carefully placed it on the table.

"Wow!" Eric said. "Look at the size of that bone."

"It must be from the Brachiosaurus," Cam said, "the one they were fixing in the museum."

The Milkman walked through the open door and into the house.

"They'll probably use plaster of Paris to make a copy of the bone," Cam said. "They'll take the copy to the museum tomorrow and leave it there in place of the real one."

"But how do they get in and out of the museum?" Eric asked.

"And why do they want the bones?" Cam added.

Cam and Eric stopped talking. They heard the front door of the house open and then slam shut.

After a few minutes Cam whispered, "I didn't hear the truck drive away, but they should be gone by now. Let's take a look."

Cam walked quietly. Eric followed her. Cam peeked out past the edge of the garage wall. She saw that the truck was still in the driveway. And she saw something else.

"Our bicycles," Cam said. "What if *they* see them!"

"We sure did see your bicycles," a man said.

Cam turned. It was the Milkman. He was standing behind Eric.

"Janet!" the Milkman called.

A woman came out. She was wearing a purple dress. It was Janet Tyler, the museum guide.

"Well, well," she said. "Look who we have here. It's the Click, Click Girl and her friend."

The Milkman put a key into a lock at the side of the garage door. The lock was electric. He turned the key and the door opened.

The Milkman led Cam and Eric into the garage. He pressed a button on the wall. The garage door closed.

Janet Tyler and the Milkman started to argue. She pointed to the dinosaur bones on the table.

"It's all over. We'll have to give these back. And it's your fault. You should have made copies of the three bones last night. Then these kids wouldn't have followed us."

"I'm not giving anything back. Not yet," the Milkman said. "We'll do just as we planned. We'll take the bones along on our dinosaur hunt. We'll bury them and then dig them up. *Then* we'll give the bones back to the museum."

Janet closed her eyes and said, "I can just see the newspaper headline: 'Janet Tyler discovers buried dinosaur bones and gives them to the museum.' I'll be famous. I'll speak to science groups all over the country. I'll make a fortune."

Cam pulled on Eric's sleeve and whispered, "This is our chance. Janet's eyes are closed. Take out the whistles you bought."

Eric reached into his pocket. He took out the two dog whistles shaped like dinosaurs. Cam took one of them.

"When I tell you to, blow the whistle," Cam whispered. "Blow it as hard as you can."

"Stop whispering," the Milkman said.

Janet opened her eyes. She seemed surprised to be in the garage with Cam, Eric, and the Milkman.

Then the Milkman told Cam and Eric, "Either you agree not to tell anyone about our plan, or we'll call the museum director. We'll put the bones in your bicycle baskets and tell the director you took them and we caught you."

Cam turned to whisper to Eric.

Janet Tyler smiled. "That's right," she said. "You talk it over with your friend."

"Quietly count to three," Cam whispered. "Then blow the whistle."

"One . . ."

Cam quickly turned around. She pressed the garage door button.

"Two . . ."

The garage door opened.

"Three."

Cam and Eric blew the whistles hard. Janet could hardly hear the sounds the whistles made. But she knew what kind of whistles they were.

"Get the bones!" Janet yelled. "Get the bones before some dog comes and runs off with them."

She opened the door to the house. The Milkman picked up as many of the bones as he could carry.

"Quick, Eric!" Cam said. "Crawl under the table."

Cam and Eric crawled under the table and ran out of the garage. A big brown dog and two smaller dogs ran past them toward the garage.

Cam and Eric ran around the milk truck to the bicycles. They got on them just as the Milkman ran out of the house.

"Stop!" he yelled.

"Let's go!" Cam said to Eric.

Cam looked both ways. No cars were coming. She quickly rode across the street. Eric followed her.

Just as they got across the street, they heard the door of the milk truck open and shut. The engine started.

Cam turned quickly and looked behind her. Eric was pedaling hard. And the milk truck was right behind Eric.

Cam pedaled as hard as she could. She signaled and turned the corner. Eric followed her.

"Screech!"

"Honk! Honk!"

Cam stopped pedaling and turned to see what was happening. A car had turned the corner right in front of the milk truck. Both the driver of the car and the Milkman had slammed on their brakes.

"This is our chance," Cam told Eric.

Cam and Eric were riding on a busy street now. There were stores on both sides of the street.

Cam saw a narrow path on the side of a store. She rode down the path to the back of the store. Eric followed her.

"Good thinking," Eric said once they had stopped their bicycles. "When the Milkman turns the corner, he won't be able to find us."

Cam got off her bicycle. Then she told Eric, "I'm going inside to call the museum."

Cam said "Click" to help her remember the museum's number. Then she dialed.

"This is Cam Jansen," Cam said to the director. "I'm the girl who was found hiding in the dinosaur room after the museum closed."

Cam told the director about the Milkman, Janet Tyler, and the dinosaur bones. She also told him the name and address of the store. "Yes, we'll wait here for you," Cam said, and then she hung up.

Soon a car drove up and stopped in front of the store. The director was at the wheel. He waved to Cam and Eric. They got on their bicycles. The director followed them in his car to the small brick house with the white wooden fence. The milk truck was in the driveway again.

"This is it," Cam told the director.

"You don't have to worry about the bones," the director said. "Since I know Janet stole them, she can't bury the bones and pretend to discover them. The bones are no good to her any more, so I'm sure she'll give them back without any trouble."

The museum director got out of his car. "Of course, she'll lose her job and I'll have to report her and her friend to the police. But they should have known that could happen when they took the bones."

The museum director shook hands with Cam and Eric. "I want to thank both of you for all your help," he said. "Before you go, you must tell me how you knew that some bones were missing. I pass those skeletons all the time, and I didn't notice anything."

Cam explained, "The last time I was at the museum, I took a picture of the dinosaur skeleton. When I looked at the picture, I knew some bones were missing."

"But our guards don't let anyone take photographs in the museum."

"Cam's camera is different," said Eric. "She doesn't need film or a flash. Cam's camera is her memory."

The director smiled. "Well, we certainly won't stop your memory from taking photographs." He buttoned his jacket, and then he asked, "Can you take one of me?"

Cam laughed. Then she looked straight at the museum director and said, "*Click.*"

Questions

1. What was Janet Tyler planning to do with the dinosaur bones?

2. Why did Cam and Eric have to escape from the Milkman and Janet?

3. Do you think Cam and Eric should have gotten the museum director's help sooner? Why or why not?

4. If you had a memory, or mental camera, like Cam's, what things would you take "pictures" of?

Applying Reading Skills
Draw Conclusions

Use complete sentences to answer the following questions about "Cam Jansen and the Mystery of the Dinosaur Bones."

1. Why did Cam conclude that some bones were missing from the tail of one of the dinosaurs at the museum?

2. Why did Cam conclude that the thieves would use plaster of Paris to make a copy of the bone?

3. Why did Janet Tyler conclude that she would be famous?

4. Why did Eric and Cam conclude that their dog whistles would help them?

WRITING activity

MYSTERY

Prewrite

A dangerous trap, a clever escape, a fast chase! What kind of story has all these events in the plot? A mystery, of course! "Cam Jansen and the Mystery of the Dinosaur Bones" is a science mystery. The story uses science facts and a science setting.

You are going to write a mystery. It can be a science or a history mystery or an everyday mystery. Before you begin to write, you must make a plan. This list gives you some ideas:

1. *Main Character* The main character of a mystery is usually a detective. Cam Jansen, a person you make up, or even you could be your main character.
2. *Problem* A mystery always has a problem that is the main idea of the story. Cam Jansen's problem was finding the missing dinosaur bones. You must decide on a problem for your mystery.
3. *Clues* Clues help the reader solve the problem. The milk truck and the bones were the clues for Cam Jansen. Remember that your clues must fit together to solve the problem.
4. *Other Needs* Plan characters, setting, and the order of events in your plot.
5. *Facts* If you are writing a history or a science mystery, you must use correct facts.

Write

1. Read the plan for your mystery again.
2. The first part should introduce the characters, setting, and the problem.
3. The second part should present your clues as part of the events in the plot.
4. The last part should solve the problem. The main character, your detective, should explain how he or she solved the problem.
5. Try to use Vocabulary Treasures in your mystery.
6. Now write the first draft of your mystery.

VOCABULARY TREASURES	
argue	rely
caution	threaten

Revise

Read your mystery again. Have a friend read it, too. Think about this checklist as you revise.

1. Check over your clues. If a reader doesn't read the end of your mystery, could he or she solve it with just the clues you gave?
2. Do your characters seem like real people? Read their conversations aloud. Do they sound real? What can you do to make them more real?
3. In the end does your main character explain how he or she solves the mystery? Does it make sense? Do you need to change anything?
4. Check the punctuation in all your sentences.
5. Now rewrite your mystery to share.

THE **VOYAGE** OF THE

MIMI

Bank Street College Project in Science and Mathematics

It is hard to believe that an animal that is bigger than the biggest dinosaur exists. It's true. Blue whales, which swim the oceans today, are the largest animals ever known.

This story is about two scientists, Dr. Anne Abrams, an oceanographer, and Dr. Ramon Rojas, a marine biologist. They are looking for another kind of whale, the humpback. They have hired the Mimi and her owner, Captain Granville, to take them out into the Atlantic Ocean. C.T., Captain Granville's grandson, will spend the summer aboard the Mimi. Three teenagers, Sally Ruth, Rachel, and Arthur, will make up the Mimi's crew. Read to see what they learn about whales.

As the *Mimi* motored out of the harbor, C.T. talked with his grandfather.

"Are we going to see whales today, Grandpa?"

"You'll have to ask Dr. Abrams," said the Captain.

"You mean Anne?" C.T. asked. Then he added, "She said I could call her that."

But Captain Granville had no more time to talk.

"All hands on deck! Let's make sail!" he called out.

At last the *Mimi* cut through the water under full sail. Everyone cheered.

"What happens now?" Arthur asked.

They all turned to the Captain for his answer. "Lunch."

In the galley, C.T. and Sally Ruth made sandwiches. When C.T. saw the peanut butter, he was amazed—a 25-pound jug! "This will last a year!"

After lunch, the crew was called below for a meeting. Anne and Ramón thought they might see whales soon because they were nearing Stellwagen Bank. It would be important that everyone know the goals of the voyage. Anne reminded them. "We'll be looking at the ways humpback whales behave. We want to identify different humpbacks, and count them."

Rachel joked, "Is that all?"

Ramón was an expert on humpbacks. "They are just returning from their winter mating grounds in the Caribbean Sea. They haven't eaten much for four months. They are HUNGRY!"

He pointed to a chart of all kinds of whales. "You can tell if a whale is a humpback by its long white flippers and its bumpy head. You can look at its chin, the shape of the fin on its back, and the black and white pattern on its tail."

Sally Ruth reminded Ramón that whales might be near. She went up to the crow's nest to be the lookout.

"If you couldn't tell one whale from another, it would be hard to learn anything about their movements and their habits," Anne pointed out.

Rachel wasn't sure. "Can you really tell one whale from another?"

Ramón nodded. "You do it by looking at a part of the tail called the flukes. The pattern on the underside of a whale's flukes is like a fingerprint. It's different for every whale. If you get a good photograph of the fluke pattern, you can try to match it with photos in this catalogue." He held up a thick book. "If you get a match, you can identify your whale."

Arthur looked through the book. "Each whale has a number."

"Yes. And some have names."

Just then C.T. stuck his head into the room. "Sally Ruth says there are whales two miles ahead!"

Rachel and Arthur scrambled up the ladder. But all they saw was ocean, no whales. They must have dived.

C.T. looked out impatiently. "How long do they stay under?" he asked Anne.

"Five or ten minutes—even more."

Suddenly, 50 meters off *Mimi*'s bow, a humpback whale leaped into the air. It crashed down on its back onto the ocean surface!

Arthur and Rachel were so excited. They almost forgot that they were there to study, not just watch. But Ramón and Anne reminded them.

"That was what we call a breach," Ramón said.

"We don't know why they do it. We've seen them breach as many as fifty times in a row," Anne added.

"There are at least three adults, maybe five," Ramón noted. "It's hard to tell."

The whales were awesome. When another whale breached, C.T. called out, "Hey, Grandpa! Look at that one!"

Anne and Rachel watched the whales. They
told Arthur about the whales' markings and
about what the whales did. Arthur tried to keep
a record. It wasn't easy when things were
happening so fast. "What if I get behind?" Arthur
wanted to know.

Ramón laughed. "We'll throw you overboard!"

Two whales started lobtailing. With their
bodies straight down in the water and only their
flukes showing, they slapped their tails down on
the ocean surface again and again.

Rachel was a little worried. "Are they mad
at us?"

Anne didn't think so. "We've seen them do
this from a long way off, so it may not be because
of us. We don't really know why they lobtail."

No matter why, it was a great chance to see
and photograph the undersides of their flukes.
Ramón thought he recognized one of the whales.
"We'll know when we develop the film," he said.

The crew watched the whales for the rest of the afternoon. Only the setting of the sun stopped their work.

Later, Sally Ruth developed the day's photographs. She showed them to the other members of the crew.

One of Ramon's photographs was of a whale that he knew from other trips. Ramón made a contest out of matching that photo to the fluke shots in the book.

"First one to match the photo with the right fluke shot in the catalogue . . ."

". . . gets out of doing the dishes for a week!" said Arthur.

"It's a deal!"

The kids raced through the catalogue. C.T. thought he spotted the match. "Here it is! 0159!" But Arthur and Rachel paid no attention. They had decided that all the patterns looked the same.

"There are over a thousand of those things," cried Arthur.

Rachel thought they had been fooled. "Nice trick, Ramón."

At the same time, Anne had taken another copy of the photograph. She was working with it at the computer. "Hey, what's that?" Arthur asked.

Anne explained. "It's a program we're working on to help us identify whales." She pointed to the drawing of the flukes on the computer screen. "The flukes are divided into fourteen areas. For each area, I look at the photograph. Then I tell the computer if the area is mostly black or white. I also tell if it has any markings."

Arthur was catching on. "And the computer stores the same information that's in the fluke catalogue?"

"Right! The computer quickly compares all the information for all the areas. It gives us a list of the most likely matches. We still have to make the final choices by eye."

"Here's the computer's list," Anne said. She punched a key and up came a list of numbers. At the top was 0159.

"Hey, look! I told you!" C.T. cried.

Sally Ruth knew it all along. "He's right. That's 'Fringe,' 0159."

Ramón nodded. "We've seen her three years in a row."

"Yahoo!" shouted C.T. "No dishes for a week!"

This was too much for Rachel. "Get out of here, you lucky kid!" But she couldn't help smiling.

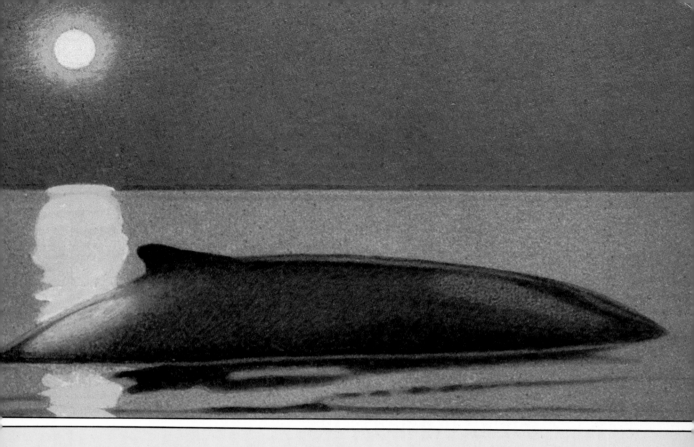

It had been a long and exciting day. *Mimi*
rode quietly on the calm sea. Everyone except
Captain Granville had turned in. But it was hard
to sleep.

Arthur's head spun with everything he'd
learned on his first day at sea. "I can't wait 'til
tomorrow."

C.T. said, "I wonder if we'll see more
whales."

The boat creaked and rocked gently. Ramón
smiled. "You never know. G'night, you guys.
Good job today."

Questions

1. What are flukes and how do they help tell one whale from another?

2. Why do whale watchers make up names for the things whales do?

3. Do you think it was just luck that C.T. matched the fluke photograph? Why or why not?

4. Pretend you had been on the *Mimi* with the others. Write a record entry describing some of the things you saw.

Applying Reading Skills
Main Idea

Read the following paragraph from "The Voyage of the Mimi." Then write the main idea of the paragraph in your own words.

Whales can be identified by the part of their tail called the flukes. The pattern on the underside of a whale's flukes is like a footprint. It is different for every whale. If you get a good photograph of the fluke pattern, you can try to match it with photographs in a catalogue.

SOUNDS FISHY!

Where do you think you could find a horse, a hatchet, a leaf, a dog, and a box? In water, of course. The oceans, rivers, and lakes have a huge amount of life in them and many of the fish are unusual looking and have unusual names. Look at the pictures of the fish named.

sea horse   hatchet fish   leaf fish   dog fish   box fish

Look at this picture of a puffer who is happy.

Now look at this picture of a puffer when it is scared.

When a puffer is in danger, it puffs itself up until it is too big to eat.

Draw pictures of four imaginary fish on your paper. Choose one fish to look like another animal, one fish to look like something that isn't alive, one fish who does something strange, and a fish you would like for a pet. Write names for all your fish.

AMOS & BORIS
WILLIAM STEIG

How can you learn about animals? Sometimes it takes observing with all your senses. It also takes imagining to learn what life is like for a snail or a whale.

In this story, a mouse that lives on land meets a whale that lives in the sea. What will such a pair think of one another? Read about the friendship that grows between these two mammals. What kind of friendship could two such different animals enjoy?

Amos, a mouse, lived by the ocean.
He loved the ocean.
He loved the smell of sea air. He loved to hear the surf sounds—the bursting breakers, the backwashes with rolling pebbles.

He thought a lot about the ocean, and he wondered about the faraway places on the other side of the water. One day he started building a boat on the beach. He worked on it in the daytime, while at night he studied navigation.

When the boat was finished, he loaded it with cheese, biscuits, acorns, honey, wheat germ, two barrels of fresh water, a compass, a sextant, a telescope, a saw, a hammer and nails and some wood in case repairs should be necessary, a needle and thread for the mending of torn sails, and various other necessities such as bandages and iodine, a yo-yo and playing cards.

On the sixth of September, with a very calm sea, he waited till the high tide had almost reached his boat; then, using his most savage strength, he just managed to push the boat into the water, climb on board, and set sail.

The *Rodent*, for that was the boat's name, proved to be very well made and very well suited to the sea. And Amos, after one miserable day of seasickness, proved to be a natural sailor, very well suited to the ship.

He was enjoying his trip immensely. It was beautiful weather. Day and night he moved up and down, up and down, on waves as big as mountains, and he was full of wonder, full of enterprise, and full of love for life.

One night, in a phosphorescent sea, he marveled at the sight of some whales spouting luminous water; and later, lying on the deck of his boat gazing at the immense, starry sky, the tiny mouse Amos, a little speck of a living thing in the vast living universe, felt thoroughly akin to it all. Overwhelmed by the beauty and mystery of everything, he rolled over and over and right off the deck of his boat and into the sea.

"Help!" he squeaked as he grabbed desperately at the *Rodent*. But it evaded his grasp and went bowling along under full sail, and he never saw it again.

349

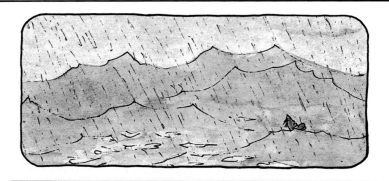

And there he was! Where? In the middle of the immense ocean, a thousand miles from the nearest shore, with no one else in sight as far as the eye could see and not even so much as a stick of driftwood to hold on to. "Should I try to swim home?" Amos wondered. "Or should I just try to stay afloat?" He might swim a mile, but never a thousand. He decided to just keep afloat, treading water and hoping that something—who knows what?—would turn up to save him. But what if a shark, or some big fish, a horse mackerel, turned up? What was he supposed to do to protect himself? He didn't know.

Morning came, as it always does. He was getting terribly tired. He was a very small, very cold, very wet and worried mouse. There was still nothing in sight but the empty sea. Then, as if things weren't bad enough, it began to rain.

At last the rain stopped and the noonday sun gave him a bit of cheer and warmth in the vast loneliness; but his strength was giving out. He began to wonder what it would be like to drown. Would it take very long? Would it feel just awful?

As he was asking himself these dreadful questions, a huge head burst through the surface of the water and loomed up over him. It was a whale. "What sort of fish are you?" the whale asked. "You must be one of a kind!"

"I'm not a fish," said Amos. "I'm a mouse, which is a mammal, the highest form of life. I live on land."

"Holy clam and cuttlefish!" said the whale. "I'm a mammal myself, though I live in the sea. Call me Boris," he added.

Amos introduced himself and told Boris how he came to be there in the middle of the ocean. The whale said he would be happy to take Amos to the Ivory Coast of Africa, where he happened to be headed anyway, to attend a meeting of whales from all the seven seas. But Amos said he'd had enough adventure to last him a while. He wanted only to get back home and hoped the whale wouldn't mind going out of his way to take him there.

"Not only would I not mind," said Boris, "I would consider it a privilege. What other whale in all the world ever had the chance to get to know such a strange creature as you! Please climb aboard." And Amos got on Boris's back.

"Are you sure you're a mammal?" Amos asked. "You smell more like a fish." Then Boris the whale went swimming along, with Amos the mouse on his back.

What a relief to be so safe, so secure again! Amos lay down in the sun, and being worn to a frazzle, he was soon asleep.

Then all of a sudden he was in the water again, wide awake, spluttering and splashing about! Boris had forgotten for a moment that he had a passenger on his back and had sounded. When he realized his mistake, he surfaced so quickly that Amos was sent somersaulting, tail over whiskers, high into the air.

Hitting the water hurt. In rage, Amos screamed and punched at Boris until he remembered he owed his life to the whale and quietly climbed on his back. From then on, whenever Boris wanted to sound, he warned Amos in advance and got his okay, and whenever he sounded, Amos took a swim.

Swimming along, sometimes at great speed, sometimes slowly and leisurely, sometimes resting and exchanging ideas, sometimes stopping to sleep, it took them a week to reach Amos's home shore. During that time, they developed a deep admiration for one another. Boris admired the delicacy, the quivering daintiness, the light touch, the small voice, the gemlike radiance of the mouse. Amos admired the bulk, the grandeur, the power, the purpose, the rich voice, and the abounding friendliness of the whale.

They became the closest possible friends. They told each other about their lives, their ambitions. They shared their deepest secrets with each other. The whale was very curious about life on land and was sorry that he could never experience it. Amos was fascinated by the whale's accounts of what went on deep under the sea. Amos sometimes enjoyed running up and down on the whale's back for exercise. When he was hungry, he ate plankton. The only thing he missed was fresh, unsalty water.

The time came to say goodbye. They were at the shore. "I wish we could be friends forever," said Boris. "We *will* be friends forever, but we can't be together. You must live on land and I must live at sea. I'll never forget you, though."

"**A**nd you can be sure I'll never forget *you*," said Amos. "I will always be grateful to you for saving my life and I want you to remember that if you ever need my help I'd be more than glad to give it!" How he could ever possibly help Boris, Amos didn't know, but he knew how willing he was.

The whale couldn't take Amos all the way in to land. They said their last goodbye and Amos dived off Boris's back and swam to the sand.

From the top of a cliff he watched Boris spout twice and disappear.

Boris laughed to himself. "How could that little mouse ever help me? Little as he is, he's all heart. I love him, and I'll miss him terribly."

Boris went to the conference off the Ivory Coast of Africa and then went back to a life of whaling about, while Amos returned to his life of mousing around. And they were both happy.

Many years after the incidents just described, when Amos was no longer a very young mouse, and when Boris was no longer a very young whale, there occurred one of the worst storms of the century, Hurricane Yetta; and it just so happened that Boris the whale was flung ashore by a tidal wave and stranded on the very shore where Amos happened to make his home.

It also just so happened that when the storm had cleared up and Boris was lying high and dry on the sand, losing his moisture in the hot sun and needing desperately to be back in the water, Amos came down to the beach to see how much damage Hurricane Yetta had done. Of course Boris and Amos recognized each other at once. I don't have to tell you how these old friends felt at meeting again in this desperate situation. Amos rushed toward Boris. Boris could only look at Amos.

"Amos, help me," said the mountain of a whale to the mote of a mouse. "I think I'll die if I don't get back in the water soon." Amos gazed at Boris in an agony of pity. He realized he had to do something very fast and had to think very fast about what it was he had to do. Suddenly he was gone.

357

"**I**m afraid he won't be able to help me," said Boris to himself. "Much as he wants to do something, what can such a little fellow do?"

Just as Amos had once felt, all alone in the middle of the ocean, Boris felt now, lying on the shore. He was sure he would die. And just as he was preparing to die, Amos came racing back with two of the biggest elephants he could find.

Without wasting time, these two goodhearted elephants got to pushing with all their might at Boris's huge body until he began turning over, breaded with sand, and rolling down toward the sea. Amos, standing on the head of one of the elephants, yelled instructions, but no one heard him.

In a few minutes Boris was already in water, with waves washing at him, and he was feeling the wonderful wetness. "You have to be *out* of the sea really to know how good it is to be *in* it," he thought. "That is, if you're a whale." Soon he was able to wiggle and wriggle into deeper water.

He looked back at Amos on the elephant's head. Tears were rolling down the great whale's cheeks. The tiny mouse had tears in his eyes, too. "Goodbye, dear friend," squeaked Amos. "Goodbye, dear friend," rumbled Boris, and he disappeared in the waves. They knew they might never meet again. They knew they would never forget each other.

Snails to Whales

You can learn about animals and nature by reading and observing. In *Snails to Whales*, you read about what animals look like and what they eat. You even learned how to observe some animals in their natural environments. Maybe after reading *Snails to Whales*, your understanding of nature has grown.

Thinking About *Snails to Whales*

1. How did Jim Arnosky in "Secrets of a Wildlife Watcher," Simon in "A Salmon for Simon," and Abbey and Grandma in "My Island Grandma" show respect for animals?

2. What kinds of food does a meadow mouse eat? What does a grizzly bear eat?

3. What are some ways people can help animals in a cold winter?

4. Why do you think people are so interested in finding out about dinosaurs?

5. Write about why *Snails to Whales* is a good name for this unit. Use examples from the stories in your answer.

Glossary

This glossary can help you to pronounce and find out the meanings of words in this book that you may not know.

The words are listed in alphabetical order. Guide words at the top of each page tell you the first and last words on the page.

Each word is divided into syllables. The way to pronounce each word is given next. You can understand the pronunciation respelling by using the key on the next page. A shorter key appears at the bottom of every other page.

When a word has more than one syllable, a dark accent mark (') shows which syllable is stressed. In some words, a light accent mark (') shows which syllable has a less heavy stress.

The following abbreviations are used in this glossary:

n. noun	*v.* verb	*adj.* adjective
adv. adverb	*pl.* plural	*conj.* conjunction

The glossary entries were adapted from the Macmillan *Beginning Dictionary*.

PRONUNCIATION KEY

Vowel Sounds

/a/	bat	/i/	bib	/ou/	out, cow
/ā/	cake, rain, day	/ī/	kite, fly, pie,	/u/	sun, son, touch
/ä/	father		light	/ù/	book, pull, could
/är/	car	/ir/	clear, cheer, here	/ü/	moon`
/ãr/	dare, hair	/o/	top, watch	/ū/	cute, few, music
/e/	hen, bread	/ō/	rope, soap, so,	/ə/	about, taken,
/ē/	me, meat, baby,		snow		apron, helpful
	believe	/ô/	saw, song, auto		pencil
/èr/	term, first,	/oi/	coin, boy	/r/	letter, dollar,
	worm, turn	/ôr/	fork, ore, oar		doctor

Consonant Sounds

/b/	bear	/m/	map	/y/	yo-yo
/d/	dog	/n/	nest, know	/z/	zoo, eggs
/f/	fish, phone	/p/	pig	/ch/	chain, match
/g/	goat	/r/	rug, wrong	/sh/	show
/h/	house, who	/s/	city, seal	/th/	thin
/j/	jar, gem, fudge	/t/	tiger	/th/	those
/k/	car, key	/v/	van	/hw/	where
/l/	lamb	/w/	wagon	/ng/	song

A

ac·cor·di·on (ə kôr′ dē ən) *n.* a musical instrument with keys, metal reeds, and bellows. The bellows push air through the reeds to make a note.

a·corns (ā′ kôrns, ā′ kərns) *n.* the nuts of the oak tree.

Ad·i·ron·dack Moun·tains (ad′ ə ron′ dak mount′ ənz) *n.* a mountain range in northern New York State.

ad·mi·ra·tion (ad′ mə rā′ shə n) *n.* a feeling of approval or respect.

Af·ri·ca (af′ ri kə) *n.* a continent south of Europe, between the Atlantic Ocean and the Indian Ocean.

A·las·ka (ə las′ kə) *n.* the largest state of the United States. It is located in the northwestern part of North America.

A·leu·tian Moun·tains (ə lü′ shən mount′ ənz) *n.* a range of mountains along the east coast of the northern part of the Alaska Peninsula, in Alaska.

al·fal·fa (al fal′ fə) *n.* a plant like clover. It has bluish-purple flowers. Alfalfa is grown as a food for cattle and other livestock.

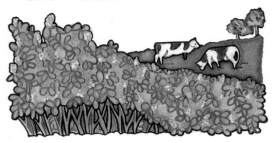

a·maze·ment (ə māz′ mənt) *n.* great surprise or wonder; astonishment.

an·cient (ān′ shənt) *adj.* having to do with times very long ago; very old.

an·gle (ang′ gəl) *n.* the space between two lines or surfaces that meet.

an·ni·ver·sa·ry (an′ ə vėr′ sər ē) *n. pl.*, **an·ni·ver·sa·ries.** the return each year of a special day. The anniversary of the day of your birth is your birthday.

Ant·arc·ti·ca (ant ärk′ ti kə, ant är′ ti kə) *n.* the continent at the South Pole.

a·pat·o·sau·rus (ə pat′ ō sôr′ əs) *n.* any of a group of very large plant-eating dinosaurs. It lived in swamplands and grew up to 80 feet in length.

ap·proach (ə prōch′) *v.* to come near or close to. *n.* the act of coming closer.

arc (ärk) *n.* **1.** an unbroken curved line between any two points on a circle. **2.** any line curving in this way.

ar·gue (är′ gū) *v.,* **ar·gued, ar·gu·ing.** to have a disagreement; quarrel.

ar·mies (är′ mēs) *n. sing.,* **army.** large, organized groups of soldiers who are armed and trained for fighting on land.

ar·tis·tic (är tis′ tik) *adj.* having to do with art or artists.

Asia (ā′ zhə) *n.* the largest continent. Asia lies between the Pacific Ocean to the east and Europe and Africa to the west.

as·pen (as′ pən) *n.* a tree whose leaves shake in the slightest breeze. An aspen is a kind of poplar.

At·las (at′ ləs) *n.* a mountain range along the northwestern coast of Africa.

at·ten·tion (ə ten′ shən) *n.* careful watching or listening.

au·di·ence (ô′ dē əns) *n.* a group of people gathered to hear or see something.

Aus·tra·lia (ôs trāl′ yə) *n.* **1.** a continent southeast of Asia, between the Indian Ocean and the Pacific Ocean. **2.** a country made up of this continent and the island of Tasmania.

au·tumn (ô′ təm) *n.* the season of the year coming between summer and winter; fall.

awe·some (ô′ səm) *adj.* inspiring overwhelming wonderment combined with fear or reverence.

B

back·stage (bak′ stāj′) *n.* the area of a theater behind the curtain line. *adj.* related to, located, or occurring backstage.

a bat, ā cake, ä father, är car, ãr dare; e hen, ē me, ėr term; i bib, ī kite, ir clear; o top, ō rope, ô saw, oi coin, ôr fork, ou out; u sun, u̇ book, ü moon, ū cute; ə about, taken

bam·boo (bam bü′) *n.* a tall, treelike plant that is related to grass.

bank (bangk) *n.* the rising ground along a river or lake.

be·have (bi hāv′) *v,* **be·haved, be·hav·ing.** to act; do.

bill·fold (bill′ fold′) *n.* a folding case for paper money.

Bim·i·ni (bim′ ə nē) *n.* two small islands of the Bahamas east of southern Florida.

bi·noc·u·lars (bə nok′ yə lərz) *n.* a device that makes distant objects look larger and closer. Binoculars are made up of two telescopes joined together, so that a person can look at distant objects with both eyes.

bi·son (bī′ sən, bī zən) *n. pl.,* **bi·son.** a large animal that has a big shaggy head with short horns and a humped back; buffalo. A bison is a wild ox. Bison are found in North America.

blis·ter (blis′ tər) *n.* a sore place on the skin that looks like a small bubble.

blood (blud) *n.* the bright red liquid that runs from a cut. Blood is pumped by the heart through the veins and arteries to all parts of the body.

bluf·fing (bluf′ ing) *v.* trying to fool someone about something.

bob·cat (bob′ kat′) *n.* a small wild cat of North America. A bobcat has reddish-brown fur with dark spots and a short tail.

brach·i·o·sau·rus (brak′ ē ō sôr′ əs) *n.* any of a group of plant-eating, very large dinosaurs that walked on four legs. It weighed up to 80 tons, and its head was about 45 feet above the ground. It was the largest land animal that ever lived.

breach (brēch) *n.* the leap of a whale out of water.

broad (brôd) *adj.* large from one side to the other side; wide.

Broad·way (brôd′ wā′) *n.* a street in New York City noted as the center of the country's theater industry.

Brook·lyn (brŭk′ lin) *n.* a borough, or part, of New York City, southeast of Manhattan, on Long Island.

Brooks River (brüks′ riv′ ər) *n.* a river flowing into Lake Naknek, in Alaska.

budge (buj) *v.,* **budged, budg·ing** move even a little.

bur·row (bẻr′ ō) *v.* to dig a hole in the ground.

bush·els (bủsh′ əlz) *n.* measures for grain, fruit, vegetables, and other dry things. One <u>bushel</u> is equal to 32 quarts.

bus·tle (bus′ əl) *n.* noisy, excited activity.

C

cam·el (kam′ əl) *n.* a large animal that has a humped back, long legs, and a long neck. <u>Camels</u> are found in deserts in northern Africa and central Asia.

cam·er·a (kam′ ər ə, kam′rə) *n.* a device for taking photographs or motion pictures.

Cap·ri·corn (kap′ rə kôrn′) *n.* a constellation in the southern sky, usually shown as a goat.

cap·tiv·i·ty (kap tiv′ ə tē) *n. pl.,* **cap·tiv·i·ties.** the state of being a captive (a person or animal captured and held in confinement).

car·di·nal (cärd′ ən əl) *n.* a songbird that has a crest of feathers on its head. The male <u>cardinal</u> has bright red feathers with a black patch around its bill.

Car·ib·be·an Sea (kar′ ə bē′ ən sē′, kə rib′ ē ən sē′) *n.* the sea bounded on the north and east by the West Indies, on the west by Central America, and on the south by South America.

car·ni·vores (kär′ nə vôrs′) *n.* animals having long, sharp teeth and sharp claws generally feeding on flesh. Dogs, lions, and bears are <u>carnivores</u>.

cast·ing (kas′ ting) *v.* the act of one who casts; choosing the actors or performers for a play or other show.

---

a bat, ā cake, ä father, är car, ãr dare; e hen, ē me, ėr term; i bib, ī kite, ir clear; o top, ō rope, ô saw, oi coin, ôr fork, ou out; u sun, ủ book, ü moon, ū cute; ə about, taken

cau·tion (kô′ shən) *n.* close care; watchfulness.

chan·nel (chan′ əl) *n.* a narrow body of water that connects two larger bodies of water.

char·ac·ters (kăr′ ik tərz) *n.* people in books, plays, stories, or motion pictures.

chir·ruped (chĕr′ əpt, chĕr′ əpt) *v.* made a sound like a continuous chirping.

chord (kôrd) *n.* a combination of three or more notes of music that are sounded at the same time to produce a harmony.

cho·rus (kôr′ əs) *n. pl.,* **cho·rus·es. 1.** a part of a song that is sung after each stanza. **2.** a group of people who sing or dance together.

churn·ing (chĕrn′ ing) *adj.* stirring or moving with a very rough motion.

chute (shüt) *n.* a steep passage or slide through which things may pass.

cin·na·mon (sin′ ə mən) *n.* a reddish-brown spice. Cinnamon is made from the dried inner bark of a tropical tree.

cir·cu·lat·ing (sĕr′ kyə lāt′ ing) *v.* moving in a circular path back to the starting point.

clo·ver (klō′ vər) *n.* a plant having leaves made up of three leaflets and rounded, fragrant flower heads of white, red, or purple flowers. Clover is used as food for cows.

cock·a·toos (kok′ ə tüs) *n.* parrots with a crest. Cockatoos are found in Australia.

co·coa (kō′kō) *n.* **1.** a brown powder made by grinding up the dried seeds of the cacao tree and removing the fat. **2.** a drink made by mixing cocoa and milk or water.

co·coon (kə kün′) *n.* the silky case that a caterpillar spins around itself. Caterpillars live in their cocoons while they are growing into moths or butterflies.

coe·lo·phy·sis (sē′lō fī′ sis) *n.* any of a group of small, light, hollow-boned dinosaurs ranging up to about 8 feet in length. It walked on two legs and was a meat-eater.

co·ho (kō′ hō) *n.* also, **co·hoe.** Short for **coho salmon,** a silver salmon.

com·mis·sar·y (kom′ ə sãr′ ē) *n. pl.,* **com·mis·sar·ies. 1.** a store that sells food and supplies. **2.** a place to eat, such as a cafeteria.

com·pa·ny (kum′ pə nē) *n. pl.,* **com·pa·nies. 1.** a guest or guests. **2.** a business firm or organization. **3.** companionship. **4.** a group of performers.

com·pas·sion (kəm pash′ ən) *n.* sympathy for someone else's suffering or misfortune, together with the desire to help.

com·plete (kəm plēt′) *adj.* thorough; perfect.

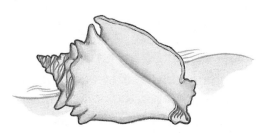

conch (congk, konch) *n. pl.,* **conch** or **conches.** the large, coiled shell of a sea animal.

con·crete (kon′ krēt, kong′ krēt, kon krēt′) *n.* a mixture of cement, pebbles, sand, and water. Concrete becomes very hard when it dries.

con·densed milk (kən denst′ milk′) *n.* cow's milk, thickened by evaporated part of the water content and sweetened with sugar.

con·fi·dence (kon′ fə dəns) *n.* **1.** faith in oneself. **2.** trust or faith.

con·serv·a·to·ry (kən sẽr′ və tôr′ ē) *n. pl.,* **con·serv·a·to·ries. 1.** a small greenhouse or glass-enclosed room for growing and displaying plants. **2.** a school for instruction in music or the fine arts.

con·tent (kən tent′) *adj.* happy and satisfied.

con·tents (kon′ tents) *n.* what something holds.

con·ven·ient (kən vēn′ yənt) *adj.* giving ease and comfort; useful; handy.

---

a bat, ā cake, ä father, är car, ãr dare; e hen, ē me, ėr term; i bib, ī kite, ir clear; o top, ō rope, ô saw, oi coin, ôr fork, ou out; u sun, u̇ book, ü moon, ū cute; ə about, taken

cork (kôrk) *n.* **1.** the light, thick, outer bark of a kind of oak tree. **2.** a stopper for a bottle or other thing, made of cork.

co·ryth·o·sau·rus (kə rith′ ō sôr′ əs) *n.* any of a group of dinosaurs that walked on two legs and lived both on land and in the water. It had webbed fingers and a hollow crest over its head. It grew to about 30 feet in length.

cos·tumes (kos′ tümz) *n.* clothes worn in order to look like someone or something else.

coursed (kôrst) *v.* moved swiftly; ran; flowed.

co·zy (kō′ zē) *adj.* warm and comfortable; snug.

cran·ber·ries (kran′ bãr′ ēz) *n. sing.*, **cran·ber·ry.** sour, red berries that grow on low shrubs and bushes in bogs and swamps.

cue (kū) *n.* a signal that tells someone to begin to do something.

cu·ra·tors (kyû rā′ tərs, kyûr′ ā tərs) *n.* people in charge of all or part of the collection or exhibit in a museum, art gallery, or zoo.

Cyg·nus (sig′ nəs) *n.* a constellation in the northern sky, usually shown as a swan.

D

de·clared (di klãrd′) *v.* **1.** said strongly and firmly. **2.** announced or made something known.

de·grees (di grēs′) *n.* units for measuring temperature.

del·i·cate (del′ i kit) *adj.* **1.** fine or dainty. **2.** easily damaged; fragile. **3.** very sensitive.

de·spair (di spãr′) *v.* to give up or lose hope. *n.* a complete loss of hope.

des·per·ate (des′ pər it) *adj.* **1.** very bad or hopeless. **2.** reckless because of having no hope.

de·tached (di tacht′) *v.* unfastened and separated; took off.

de·ter·mined (di tẽr′ mind) *adj.* having one's mind made up; firm.

de·vel·op (di vel′ əp) *v.* **1.** to treat an exposed photographic film, plate, or print with a chemical so that the picture can be seen. **2.** to bring or come into being or activity; grow.

dew (dü, dū) *n.* moisture from the air that forms drops on cool surfaces. Dew gathers on grass, plants, and trees during the night.

di·a·ry (dī′ ər ē) *n. pl.*, **di·a·ries.** a written record of the things that one does each day.

dif·fi·cult (dif′ ə kult′) *adj.* hard to do, solve, or understand; not easy.

di·no·sau·ri·a (dī′ nə sôr′ ē ə) *n.* a group of extinct reptiles with four limbs and a long tapering tail. Members of this group ranged in size from a few feet to almost 100 feet in length.

din·o·saurs (dī′ nə sôrs′) *n.* a large group of extinct reptiles that lived millions of years ago. Some dinosaurs were the largest land animals that have ever lived.

di·rec·tor (di rek′ tər, dī rek′ tər) *n.* a person or thing that manages or controls. A person who directs a play, movie, or television show is called a director.

dis·may (dis mā′) *n.* a feeling of fear or discouragement because of danger or trouble.

dis·o·be·di·ent (dis′ ə bē′ dē ənt) *adj.* refusing or failing to obey.

drafts·per·son (drafts′ pėr′ sən) *n.* a person who draws or designs plans.

drear·y (drēr′ ē) *adj.* sad or dull; gloomy.

drums (drums) *n.* musical instruments that make a sound when they are beaten.

dwell (dwel) *v.* to live in.

E

elk (elk) *n. pl.,* **elk** or **elks.** a large deer of North America. The male elk has very large antlers.

en·coun·ter (en koun′ tər) *v.* to meet; come upon or against. *n.* a coming upon or against; meeting.

en·dure (en dùr′, en dyùr′) *v.,* **en·dured, en·dur·ing.** to bear; stand; put up with.

en·er·gy (en′ ə r jē) *n. pl.,* **en·er·gies.** the strength or eagerness to work or do things.

en·ter·tain (en′ tər tān′) *v.* to keep interested and amused.

en·ve·lope (en′ və lōp′, än′ və lōp′) *n.* a flat covering or container made of paper. Envelopes are used for mailing letters and other papers.

---

a bat, ā cake, ä father, är car, âr dare; e hen, ē me, ėr term; i bib, ī kite, ir clear; o top, ō rope, ô saw, oi coin, ôr fork, ou out; u sun, ù book, ü moon, ū cute; ə about, taken

e·qual (ē′ kwəl) *adj.* that is the same in amount, number, size, or value.

eu·ca·lyp·tus (ū′ kə lip′ təs) *n. pl.*, **eu·ca·lyp·tus·es.** a tall tree that grows in warm climates. Its hard wood is used to make floors, ships, and buildings. Oil made from its leaves is used in medicine.

ex·hib·it (eg zib′ it) *n.* something shown. *v.* to show.

ex·hib·it·ed (ig zib′ it id) *v.* shown.

ex·pe·ri·ence (eks pēr′ ē əns) *n.* something that a person has done, seen, or taken part in.

ex·plor·er (eks plôr′ ər) *n.* a person who explores.

ex·posed (eks pōzd′) *adj.* left open or without protection.

ex·tinct (eks tingkt′) *adj.* no longer existing.

F

far·a·way (fär′ ə wā′) *adj.* at a great distance; remote.

fi·ber·glass (fī′ bər glas′) *n.* a strong material that is made of fine threads of glass.

fid·dle (fid′ əl) *n.* a violin.

fig·ure·heads (fig′ yər hedz′) *n.* carved wooden figures placed on the bows of ships for decoration.

fire·plugs (fī r plugz) *n.* hydrants.

flukes (flüks) *n.* the lobes, or horizontal fins, of a whale's tail.

flute (flüt) *n.* a long, thin musical instrument. A person plays a flute by holding it out to one side and blowing across a hole at one end. The player makes different notes by covering the holes with the fingers or by pushing down keys that cover the holes.

fo·cused (fō′ kəst) *v.* **1.** brought to a meeting point or focus. **2.** brought into focus so as to make a clear image.

fos·sils (fos′ əls) *n.* remains or traces of animals or plants that lived long ago.

fringe (frinj) *n.* a border of hanging threads or cord.

fu·ri·ous (fūr′ ē əs) *adj.* very angry.

G

gai·ly (gā′ lē) *adv.* in a gay manner; happily; cheerfully.

gal·ley (gal′ ē) *n.* the kitchen of a ship or airplane.

gar·ter snake (gär′ tər snāk′) *n.* a snake that is green or brown with yellow stripes. It is harmless to people.

ge·ol·o·gist (jē ol′ ə jist) *n.* an expert in or student of geology.

giz·zards (giz′ ərds) *n.* the second and muscular parts of the stomachs of birds, in which partly digested food from the first parts of the stomachs is finely ground.

glis·tened (glis′ ənd) *v.* shone with bright flashes; sparkled.

gloom·i·ly (glüm′ ə lē) *adv.* in a sad or sorrowful way.

glo·ry (glôr′ ē) *n. pl.*, **glo·ries. 1.** great beauty; splendor; magnificence. **2.** great praise; honor; fame.

goal (gōl) *n.* something that a person wants and tries to get or become; aim; purpose.

golden (gōld′ ən) *adj.* **1.** made of or containing gold. **2.** having the color or shine of gold; bright or shining.

gran·o·la (grə nō′ lə) *n.* a prepared breakfast cereal or rolled oats, wheat germ, sesame seeds, brown sugar or honey, bits of dried fruit or nuts, etc.

grap·ple (grap′ əl) *n.* a grappling iron, a device with one or more hooks or clamps, used for grasping or holding something.

greed·y (grē′ dē) *adj.* having a great and selfish desire for more than one's share of something.

grove (grōv) *n.* a group of trees standing together.

gui·tar (gi tär′) *n.* a musical instrument with a long neck and six or more strings. It is played by plucking or strumming the strings.

H

hand·some (han′ səm) *adj.* having a pleasing appearance; good-looking.

ha·zel·nut (hā′ zəl nut′) *n.* the light brown, round or oval nut of the hazel tree.

herbs (hĕrbz, ĕrbz) *n.* plants whose leaves, stems, seeds, or roots are used in cooking for flavoring or in medicines.

---

a bat, ā cake, ä father, är car, âr dare; e hen, ē me, ėr term; i bib, ī kite, ir clear; o top, ō rope, ô saw, oi coin, ôr fork, ou out; u sun, u̇ book, ü moon, ū cute; ə about, taken

her·mit crab (hĕr′ mit krab′) *n.* any of a certain kind of ocean-dwelling crabs that occupy the empty shells of snails, whelks, and similar animals, for protection.

hes·i·tat·ed (hez′ ə tāt′ id) *v.* waited or stopped a moment.

hi·ber·na·tion (hī′ bər nā′ shən) *n.* the inactive or sleeping state in which some animals spend part of the winter.

hordes (hôrds) *n.* very large groups.

hump·back (hump′ bak′) *n.* a black-and-white whale having a rounded back and long, knobby flippers.

hut (hut) *n.* a small, roughly built house or shelter.

hy·drant (hī′ drənt) *n.* a wide, covered pipe that sticks out of the ground and is attached to a water main. Fire hoses are attached to hydrants to get water to put out fires.

I

i·den·ti·fy (ī den′ tə fī′) *v.,* **i·den·ti·fied, i·den·ti·fy·ing.** to show or prove that a person or thing is who or what you say it is.

i·guan·o·don (i gwä′ nə don′) *n.* any of a group of plant-eating dinosaurs that walked on two feet. It grew to a height of about 15 feet.

im·pa·tient·ly (im pā′ shənt lē) *adv.* in a manner showing inability to put up with delay or opposition calmly and without anger.

im·pris·oned (im priz′ ənd) *v.* put or kept in prison; locked up.

in·clud·ed (in klüd′ id) *v.* had as part of the whole; contained.

in·crease (in krēs′) *v.,* **in·creased, in·creas·ing.** to make or become greater in number or size.

in·di·vid·u·al (in′ də vij′ ü əl) *adj.* single, separate. *n.* a single person or thing.

in·fin·i·ty (in fin′ ə tē) *n. pl.,* **in·fin·i·ties. 1.** boundlessness. **2.** indefinitely or extremely great amount or number.

in·stru·ment (in′ strə mənt) *n.* **1.** a device for producing musical sounds. **2.** a device used for doing a certain kind of work; tool.

in·su·lat·ed (in′ sə lāt′ id) *adj.* covered or surrounded with material that slows or stops the flow of electricity, heat, or sound.

in·sult (*verb*, in sult′; *noun*, in′ sult) *v.* to speak to or treat in a way that hurts or angers. *n.* a remark or action that hurts or angers.

in·tent (in tent′) *adj.* having the mind firmly fixed on something.

in·vis·i·ble (in viz′ ə bəl) *adj.* not able to be seen; not visible.

in·vit·ed (in vīt′ id) *v.* asked someone to go somewhere or to do something.

isle (īl) *n.* an island. <u>Isles</u> are usually small islands.

J

jas·mine (jaz′ min, jas′ min) *n.* the fragrant bell-shaped flower of any of a large group of plants of the olive family, growing in yellow, white, or pink.

jew·els (jü′ əlz) *n.* precious stones; gems.

K

kale (kāl) *n.* the broad, curly, bluish-green leaves of a plant of the cabbage family.

Kat·mai (kat′ mī) *n.* the name of a national park and volcanic mountain in Alaska, on the Alaska Peninsula.

kiln (kiln, kil) *n.* a furnace or oven for burning, baking, or drying. A <u>kiln</u> is used in making bricks, pottery, and charcoal.

L

la·bels (lā′ bəls) *n.* pieces of cloth, paper, or other material fastened to something.

Lake Nak·nek (lāk′ nak′ nek′) *n.* a lake in Alaska, near the northern end of the Alaska Peninsula. <u>Lake Naknek</u> lies almost entirely within Katmai National Park.

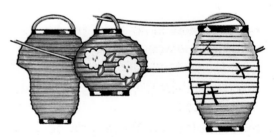

lan·terns (lan′ tərns) *n.* coverings for lights. Some lanterns are made of metal with sides of glass. Most <u>lanterns</u> can be carried.

---

a bat, ā cake, ä father, är car, âr dare; e hen, ē me, ėr term; i bib, ī kite, ir clear; o top, ō rope, ô saw, oi coin, ôr fork, ou out; u sun, u̇ book, ü moon, ū cute; ə about, taken

lar·der (lär′ dər) *n.* a place where food is kept; pantry.

lav·en·der (lav′ ən dər) *n.* a light-purple color. *adj.* having the color lavender; light purple.

leg·ends (lej′ ənds) *n.* stories passed down through the years that many people have believed, but that are not entirely true.

loaf (lōf) *n.* baked bread in one piece.

lob·tail (lob′ tāl′) *v.* to hit or slap the surface of the water with the tail. Said of whales.

lo·cal (lō′ kəl) *adj.* having to do with a particular place.

lo·tus-eat·ers (lō′ təs ē′ tərs) *n.* men in Greek legend who ate lotus fruit and led lives of ease and forgetfulness.

lunged (lunjd) *v.* moved forward suddenly.

lu·pine (lü′ pin) *n.* any of a certain group of plants of the pea family, bearing spikes of white, yellow, blue, or purple flowers.

Ly·ra (lī′ rə) *n.* a constellation in the northern sky, including the bright star Vega, usually shown as a harp.

M

mad·ame (mə dam′, ma dam′, mad′ əm) *n. pl.,* **mes·dames.** lady; mistress. Used as a form of respectful address for a married woman; also used as a title of distinction.

mam·mals (mam′ əlz) *n.* animals that are warm-blooded and have a backbone. Most mammals are covered with fur or have some hair. Female mammals have glands that produce milk, which they feed to their young. People, dogs, and whales are mammals.

man·ag·er (man′ i jər) *n.* a person who manages something.

Mar·got River (mär′ gō riv′ ər) *n.* a river in Katmai National Park, in Alaska.

ma·rine bi·ol·o·gist (mə rēn′ bī ol′ ə jist) *n.* a person who studies the plant and animal life of the sea.

marsh·land (märsh′land′) *n.* low, wet land. Grasses and reeds grow in marshlands.

mas·ter·piece (mas′ tər pēs′) *n.* something that is done with great skill and craftsmanship.

meas·ure·ment (mezh′ ər mənt) *n.* something found by measuring; the size, height, or amount of something.

Med·i·ter·ra·ne·an (med′ ə tə rā′ nē ən) *n.* a large sea between southern Europe, western Asia, and northern Africa.

men·tal (ment′ əl) *adj.* done by or having to do with the mind.

min·nows (min′ ōs) *n.* small freshwater fish.

mir·ror (mir′ ər) *n.* a smooth, polished surface that shows the image of the person or thing in front of it by reflecting light. Most mirrors are made of glass with an aluminum or silver coating on the back.

mis·er·a·bly (miz′ ər ə blē) *adv.* in a very unhappy or wretched manner.

moats (mōts) *n.* deep, wide ditches that were dug around a castle or town in former times for protection against enemies.

mol·e·cules (mol′ə kūlz) *n.* the smallest particles into which a substance can be divided and not be changed chemically. A molecule is made up of two or more atoms that are joined by a pair of shared electrons.

mon·i·tor (mon′ə tər) *n.* a student in school given a special duty or task.

mot·to (mot′ ō) *n. pl.*, **mot·toes** or **mot·tos.** a short sentence or phrase that says what someone believes or what something stands for.

Mount Ka·to·li·nat (mount′ kə tō′ li nat) *n.* a volcanic mountain in Katmai National Park, in Alaska, near Lake Naknek.

mul·ti·col·ored (mul′ ti kul′ ərd) *adj.* of many and various colors.

mu·se·ums (mū sē′ əms) *n.* buildings where objects of art, science, or history are kept and displayed for people to see.

mu·si·cal (mū′ zi kəl) *n.* a play that has songs and dancing in it. *adj.* having to do with or producing music.

---

a bat, ā cake, ä father, är car, âr dare; e hen, ē me, ėr term; i bib, ī kite, ir clear; o top, ō rope, ô saw, oi coin, ôr fork, ou out; u sun, u̇ book, ü moon, ū cute; ə about, taken

N

nas·ty (nas′ tē) *adj.* **1.** coming from hate or spite; mean. **2.** disagreeable or unpleasant.

Na·tion·al Zo·o·log·i·cal Park (nash′ ən əl zō′ə loj′ i kəl pärk′) *n.* a large zoo in Washington, D.C.

nat·u·ral·ist (nach′ ər ə list) *n.* a person who knows a great deal about plants or animals.

na·vies (nā′ vēs) *n. sing.,* **na·vy.** the men, supplies, and equipment that make up the entire sea forces of a country.

nec·es·sar·y (nes′ ə sãr′ ē) *adj.* that cannot be done without; needed; required.

nec·tar (nek′ tər) *n.* **1.** the sweet liquid formed in flowers. **2.** any sweet and delicious drink.

net·work (net′ wérk′) *n.* a system of lines or structures that cross.

North A·mer·i·ca (nôrth′ ə mãr′ i kə) *n.* a continent in the Western Hemisphere. North America lies between the Atlantic Ocean and the Pacific Ocean. It includes the countries of Mexico, the United States, and Canada.

nu·tri·tion (nü trish′ ən) *n.* food; nourishment.

O

o·be·di·ent·ly (ō bē′ dē ənt lē) *adv.* in a manner indicating willingness to obey.

oc·ca·sion·al·ly (ə kā′ shən əl ē) *adv.* once in a while; at times.

o·cean·og·ra·pher (ō′ shə nog′ rə fər) *n.* a person who studies the oceans and the animals and plants that live in them.

ol·ive-col·ored (ol′ iv kul′ ərd) *adj.* having the color olive; dull yellowish-green.

on·ions (un′ yəns) *n.* the round or oval bulbs of a plant. Onions have a strong, sharp taste and smell.

ought (ôt) *v.* should.

out·fit (out′ fit′) *n.* **1.** a set of clothes. **2.** all the articles or pieces of equipment needed for doing something.

oys·ter (ois′ tər) *n.* an animal that has a soft body and a rough, hinged shell. Oysters are found in shallow waters along coasts.

P

pa·ja·mas (pə jä′ məz, pə jam′ əz) *n.* a set of clothes to sleep in, usually made up of a shirt and trousers.

pa·le·on·tol·o·gist (pā′ lē on tol′ ə jist) *n.* an expert in the science that deals with fossils and extinct forms of life.

pan·das (pan′ dəs) *n.* large animals that look like bears. A panda has long white fur with black patches and lives in southern China.

part·ners (pärt′ nərz) *n.* people who run a business together.

pa·tient·ly (pā′ shənt lē) *adv.* in a manner having or showing patience. A patient person is able to put up with hardship, pain, trouble, or delay without getting angry or upset.

pea·cocks (pē′ koks′) *n.* large birds with beautiful tails and shiny blue feathers on their heads, necks, and bodies. The peacock's tail has bright green and gold feathers with spots like eyes on them.

ped·aled (ped′ əld) *v.* worked or used the pedals of something.

per·fect·ly (pėr′ fikt lē) *adv.*
1. completely; entirely. **2.** in an excellent way; without fault.

per·form·ance (pər fôr′ məns) *n.* a play, musical program, or something else that is done in public to entertain.

per·il·ous (pār′ ə ləs) *adj.* dangerous; full of risk or harm.

per·i·win·kles (pār′ i wing′ kəls) *n.* small sea snails found in shallow waters along the coasts of Europe and northeastern North America.

pho·tog·ra·pher (fə tog′ rə fər) *n.* a person who takes pictures for fun or as a job.

pho·to·graphs (fō′ tə grafs′) *n.* pictures that are made by using a camera.

plen·ti·ful (plen′ ti fəl) *adj.* in a large amount; more than enough.

po·lice (pə lēs′) *n.* a group of persons given power by a government to keep order and to enforce the law.

---

a bat, ā cake, ä father, är car, ãr dare; e hen, ē me, ėr term; i bib, ī kite, ir clear; o top, ō rope, ô saw, oi coin, ôr fork, ou out; u sun, u̇ book, ü moon, ū cute; ə about, taken

pon·cho (pon′ chō) *n. pl.,* **pon·chos.** a cloak made of one piece of cloth or other material. It has a hole in the middle for the head. A waterproof <u>poncho</u> is worn by soldiers and hikers to keep dry.

pon·ders (pon′ dərz) *v.* thinks about something carefully.

por·ridge (pôr′ ij) *n.* a soft food made by boiling ground grains in water or milk. <u>Porridge</u> is usually eaten for breakfast.

prep·a·ra·tion (prep′ ə rā′ shən) *n.* the act of making something ready; being made ready.

pre·served (pri zėrvd′) *v.* kept or protected.

pres·sure (presh′ ər) *n.* force caused by one thing pushing against another thing.

pret·zel (pret′ səl) *n.* a crisp food baked in the shape of a knot or stick and salted on the outside.

pre·views (prē′ vūz) *n.* showings of things ahead of time.

prin·cess (prin′ sis, prin′ ses) *n. pl.,* **prin·cess·es.** the daughter of a king or queen or the wife of a prince.

pris·on·ers (priz′ ən ərz) *n.* **1.** people who are forced to stay in prison. **2.** people who are captured by someone else; captives.

pro·duc·tion (prə duk′ shən) *n.* something that is made or created.

prows (prouz) *n.* the front parts of boats or ships; bows.

purl (pėrl) *v.* to knit with inverted stitches. *n.* an inverted stitch or row of stitches in knitting.

Q

quarries (kwôr′ ēz) *n. sing.,* **quar·ry.** places where stone is cut or blasted out.

R

rai·sins (rā′ zinz) *n.* sweet, dried grapes.

ran·ger (rān′ jər) *n.* a person whose work is looking after and guarding a forest.

rare (rãr) *adj.* **1.** unusually fine or valuable. **2.** not often happening, seen, or found.

rea·son·a·bly (rē′ zə nə blē, rēz′ nə blē) *adv.* in a manner showing or using good sense and thinking; not foolishly.

re·cess (rē′ ses, ri ses′) *n. pl.,* **re·cess·es.** a time during which work or other activity stops.

re·flec·tion (ri flek′ shən) *n.* **1.** an image given back by a reflecting surface. **2.** something that is reflected.

re·frig·er·a·tors (ri frij′ ə rā′ tərs) *n.* boxes or rooms with a cooling system. Refrigerators are used to keep food and other things from spoiling.

re·hears·als (ri hĕr′ səlz) *n.* practices in preparation for a performance.

re·la·tions (ri lā′ shəns) *n.* people who belong to the same family as another; relatives.

re·ly (ri lī′) *v.*, **re·lied, re·ly·ing.** to trust; depend.

rep·tiles (rep′ təlz, rep′ tīlz) *n.* cold-blooded animals with a backbone. Reptiles have dry, scaly skin. They move by crawling on their stomachs or creeping on short legs.

rhy·thm (rith′ əm) *n.* a regular or orderly repeating of sounds or movements.

roused (rouzd) *v.* awakened from sleep, rest, or the like.

ru·ined (rü′ ind) *v.* harmed or damaged greatly.

S

Sag·it·tar·i·us (saj′ ə tār′ ē əs) *n.* a constellation located near the horizon in the northern sky, usually shown as an archer.

sal·ad (sal′ əd) *n.* a cold dish that is made with lettuce, tomatoes, or other vegetables and often served with a dressing.

sal·a·man·ders (sal′ ə man′ dərs) *n.* animals that look like small lizards. They live in or near fresh water.

sal·mon (sam′ ə n) *n. pl.*, **sal·mon** or **sal·mons.** a large fish with a silvery body. It is used for food.

san·dals (sand′ əlz) *n.* shoes with a sole held to the foot by one or more straps.

---

a bat, ā cake, ä father, är car, âr dare; e hen, ē me, ėr term; i bib, ī kite, ir clear; o top, ō rope, ô saw, oi coin, ôr fork, ou out; u sun, u̇ book, ü moon, ū cute; ə about, taken

sat·is·fac·tion (sat′ is fak′ shən) *n.* the state of being satisfied.

scabs (skabz) *n.* crusts that form over sores or wounds.

scal·lop (skol′ əp, skal′ əp) *n.* a sea animal that is enclosed by two ridged shells. These shells close to protect the soft body inside, and open to let in food and water.

scen·er·y (sē′ nər ē) *n. pl.,* **scen·er·ies.** the painted scenes or pictures that are used to make the setting of a play or movie.

scent (sent) *n.* **1.** a smell. **2.** the trail or tracks by which someone or something can be traced or found.

scold (skōld) *v.* to find fault with; speak sharply to.

scorn·ful·ly (skôrn′ fəl ē) *adv.* in a manner showing or feeling hatred; scorn.

scowled (skould) *v.* frowned in an angry way.

scram·bled (skram′ bəld) *v.* moved or climbed quickly.

scut·ter (skut′ ər) *v.,* **scut·tered, scut·ter·ing.** to go or move with short rapid steps very hurriedly.

sea a·nem·o·nes (sē′ ə nem′ ə nēs) *n.* groups of sea animals that attach themselves to rocks, wharves, and other objects, having numerous tentacles that bear stinging cells used to stun prey.

sea·bag (sē′ bag′) *n.* a bag, usually of soft material, used by sailors to carry their clothes and other possessions.

seize (sēz) *v.,* **seized, seiz·ing** **1.** to take hold of; grab. **2.** to get control of; capture.

sen·ti·nels (sent′ ən əlz) *n.* people or animals that are stationed to keep watch and alert others of danger; guards; sentries.

Sep·tem·ber (sep tem′ bər) *n.* the ninth month of the year.

ser·vant (sėr′ vənt) *n.* a person hired to work for the comfort or protection of others.

sev·er·al (sev′ ər əl) *adj.* more than two, but not many. *n.* more than two, but not many people or things.

shal·low (shal′ ō) *adj.* not deep.

shel·lac (shə lak′) *n.* a liquid used as a varnish on floors and furniture to protect them and make them shine.

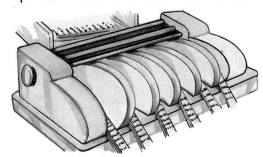

shred·ders (shred′ ərz) *n.* machines that cut or tear paper into long, narrow strips.

si·lence (sī′ ləns) *n.* a lack of sound.

si·rens (sī′ rənz) *n.* whistles with a loud, shrill sound. <u>Sirens</u> are used as signals or warnings.

skel·e·ton (skel′ ət ən) *n.* a framework of bones that supports the body of all animals with backbones.

slen·der·er (slen′ dər ər) *adj.* less big around; thinner.

slight·ly (slīt′ lē) *adv.* to a small degree or in a small amount.

South America (south′ ə mãr′ i kə) *n.* a continent in the Western Hemisphere. It is southeast of North America.

sow·ing (sō′ ing) *v.* scattering seeds over the ground.

spanned (spand) *v.* extended over or across.

spar·kle (spär′ kəl) *v.*, **spar·kled, spar·kling.** to shine in quick, bright flashes.

spar·row (spãr′ ō) *n.* a small bird with brown, white, and gray feathers and a short bill.

spe·cial·ists (spesh′ ə lists) *n.* people who know a great deal about something.

splen·did (splen′ did) *adj.* quite beautiful or magnificent.

sta·ble (stā′ bəl) *n.* a building where horses or cattle are kept and fed.

stage·hands (stāj′ handz′) *n.* in the theater, people who move scenery, set props, control lighting, and perform certain other duties.

steg·o·sau·rus (steg′ ə sôr′ əs) *n.* any of a group of plant-eating dinosaurs that walked on four legs. It had a double row of upright bony plates on its back and grew to a length of 20 to 30 feet.

---

a bat, ā cake, ä father, är car, ãr dare; e hen, ē me, ėr term; i bib, ī kite, ir clear; o top, ō rope, ô saw, oi coin, ôr fork, ou out; u sun, u̇ book, ü moon, ū cute; ə about, taken

stout·ness (stout′ nis) *n.* the state or condition of being thick and heavy, or fat.

strummed (strumd) *v.* played in an easy, relaxed, or unskilled way.

suc·cess (sək ses′) *n. pl.,* **suc·ces·ses. 1.** a person or thing that succeeds. **2.** a result that has been hoped for; a turning out well or doing well.

suit·case (süt′ kās′) *n.* a flat bag for carrying clothes when traveling.

sup·ports (sə pôrts′) *v.* hold up. *n.* **1.** the supporting of something or someone. **2.** people or things that support.

sur·face (sėr′ fis) *n.* the outside or top part of a thing.

sur·round·ed (sə roun′ did) *v.* was on all sides of; formed a circle around.

sur·viv·al (sər vī′ vəl) *n.* the act of surviving.

sur·vive (sər vīv′) *v.,* **sur·vived, sur·vi·ving.** to live longer than; live through.

sus·tain·ing (sə stān′ ing) *v.* comforting; keeping up the spirits or courage of.

swan (swon) *n.* a large water bird that has a long graceful neck and webbed feet. Swans are related to ducks and geese.

swap (swop) *v.,* **swapped, swap·ping.** to exchange; trade.

T

tal·ents (tal′ ənts) *n.* natural abilities or skills.

tal·ons (tal′ ənz) *n.* strong, sharp claws of an eagle or other bird of prey.

tarp (tärp) *n.* a short form of **tar·pau·lin** (tär pô′ lin, tar′ pə lin), waterproofed canvas or other material, as nylon, used as a protective cover for boats, athletic fields, or other objects exposed to the weather.

tell·tale (tel′ tāl′) *adj.* that reveals or shows what is not intended to be known or seen.

tem·per·a·ture (tem′ pər ə chər) *n.* the degree of heat or coldness. The temperature of a person's body or of the weather outdoors is measured by a thermometer.

tense (tens) *adj.* **1.** showing or causing strain or suspense. **2.** stretched or drawn tight; strained.

ter·rif·ic (tə rif′ ik) *adj.* extremely good; wonderful.

ter·ror (ter′ ər) *n.* great fear.

Thanks·giv·ing (thangks' giv' ing) *n.* a holiday in the United States celebrated as a day of thanksgiving and feasting. It observes the memory of the harvest feast celebrated by the Pilgrims in 1621.

ther·mo·stat (thėr' mə stat') *n.* a device that automatically controls temperature.

threat·ens (thret' əns) *v.* **1.** the cause of danger or harm. **2.** makes a threat of or against.

tis·sue pa·per (tish' ü pā'pər) *n.* a very thin paper used for wrapping or packing.

tour (tûr) *n.* a trip or journey in which many places are visited or many things are seen. *v.* to travel in or through a place.

tour·ists (tûr' ists) *n.* people who travel on a vacation.

tow·el·horse (tou' əl hôrs') *n.* a frame or structure, usually with four legs, for holding towels.

tow·ers (tou' ərs) *n.* tall and narrow structures or parts of buildings.

traf·fic (traf' ik) *n.* automobiles, airplanes, ships, or people moving along a route.

trem·bled (trem' bəld) *v.* shook with cold, fear, weakness, or anger.

tri·cer·a·tops (trī ser' ə tops') *n.* any of a group of plant-eating dinosaurs with a bony plate covering the neck. It walked on four legs and grew to lengths of 30 feet.

trop·i·cal (trop' i kəl) *adj.* having to do with or found in the tropics.

trudged (trujd) *v.* walked slowly and with an effort.

ty·ran·no·sau·rus rex (ti ran' ə sôr' əs reks', tī ran' ə sôr' əs reks') *n.* a large meat-eating dinosaur having small forelimbs and a large head. It walked on two legs, had long teeth and very sharp claws, and stood nearly 13 feet high.

U

un·der·ground (un' dər ground' *adjective and adverb;* un' dər ground' *noun*) *adv.* below the earth's surface. *adj.* below the earth's surface. *n.* a place below the earth's surface.

---

a bat, ā cake, ä father, är car, ãr dare; e hen, ē me, ėr term; i bib,
ī kite, ir clear; o top, ō rope, ô saw, oi coin, ôr fork, ou out; u sun,
u̇ book, ü moon, ū cute; ə about, taken

un·ex·pect·ed (un′ iks pek′ tid) *adj.* coming or happening without warning; not expected.

un·guard·ed (un′ gärd′ id) *adj.* **1.** not kept safe from harm or danger; unprotected. **2.** not watched over or controlled.

V

van·ished (van′ isht) *v.* went out of sight or existence; disappeared.

verse (vers) *n.* **1.** a section of a poem or song; stanza. **2.** words that are written in a particular pattern and often in rhyme; poetry.

vi·brat·ing (vī′ brāt′ ing) *v.* moving rapidly back and forth or up and down.

W

Wash·ing·ton, D. C., (wô′ shing tən, dē′ sē′; wosh′ ing tən, dē′ sē′) the city that is the capital of the United States. It lies between Maryland and northern Virginia, and includes all of the District of Columbia.

wea·sel (wē′ zəl) *n. pl.,* **wea·sels** or **wea·sel.** a small animal that has a slender body, short legs, a long neck, and soft, thick brownish fur. Weasels eat rabbits and other small animals, snakes, and small birds.

wed·ding (wed′ ing) *n.* a marriage ceremony.

went·le·trap (wen′ təl trap′) *n.* a small sea animal with a shell that is usually spiral.

wheel·bar·row (hwēl′ bãr′ ō) *n.* a small vehicle with one or two wheels at the front end and two handles at the back. Wheelbarrows are used to move sand, dirt, bricks, or other small loads.

whisk·ers (hwis′ kərs) *n.* stiff hairs that grow on the face.

wild·life (wīld′ līf′) *n.* wild animals that live naturally in an area.

wiz·ard (wiz′ ərd) *n.* a person who is thought to have magical powers.

wood·peck·ers (wŭd′ pek′ ərs) *n.* birds that have a strong pointed bill. The woodpecker uses its bill to make holes in trees in order to get insects to eat. It is found in forests throughout the world.

Z

zo·o·log·i·cal (zō′ ə loj′ i kəl) *adj.* of or relating to animals.

word work

This part of *Observing* is a review of letters and the sounds they stand for. Looking carefully at these letters will help you know how to say and read many new words.

Lessons

1 Initial Consonants

Letters stand for sounds at the beginning of words.

___ob ___ought a ___asket of ___erries.

Without the letters that make the beginning sounds, the sentence above does not make sense. What letter could you use to finish the sentence?

Number your paper from 1 to 8. Write the sentences below. Fill in the missing letters. Choose the letters from those in the box. Be sure the words make sense in the sentence.

f	p	y	v	z	m	b	l

1. The ___ebra was my favorite animal at the ___oo.
2. I always ___iked ___ions and ___eopards, too.
3. But ___esterday I saw the best animal ___et!
4. It looks much like a ___ear and eats ___amboo.
5. I was ___ery lucky to ___iew one.
6. ___ost of these ___agnificent ___ammals live in China.
7. Only a ___ew can be ___ound in the U.S.A.
8. ___erhaps you've guessed—it's a ___anda!

2 Initial Consonants

Some beginning sounds can be spelled more than one way.

Read the words below. Look at the underlined letters.

<u>h</u>ouse	<u>n</u>o	<u>r</u>ight	<u>j</u>oke	<u>s</u>ign
<u>wh</u>o	<u>kn</u>ow	<u>wr</u>ite	<u>g</u>iant	<u>c</u>ity

Number your paper from 1 to 12. Read each group of words. Write the two words from each group that begin with the same sound.

1. wrote
worth
road

2. work
whole
harbor

3. cell
caution
success

4. jewels
geologist
galley

5. knocked
needles
kernels

6. coarse
source
cereal

7. ruined
wounds
wrong

8. hesitated
whispered
wholesale

9. jasmine
general
guitar

10. kitchen
knitting
nectar

11. wrapped
warrior
reward

12. celebrate
suggested
confuse

3 Final Consonants

Letters stand for sounds at the end of words.

Read each word below. Look at the underlined letters.

cal<u>m</u>	ta<u>g</u>	bo<u>x</u>	carefu<u>l</u>	cactu<u>s</u>
migh<u>t</u>	nee<u>d</u>	aga<u>in</u>	pu<u>ll</u>	acro<u>ss</u>

Some ending sounds can be spelled in more than one way. Which word ends with the sound you hear at the end of *careful*? Which word ends with the sound you hear at the end of *cactus*?

Number your paper from 1 to 8. Copy the sentences below. Fill in the missing letters. Choose letters from those in the box.

m   g   x   l   ll   s   ss   t   d   n

1. I was sitting on a lo___ when I heard a twi___ snap.
2. I looked up and saw Tyrannosaurus Re___ about si___ yards away!
3. That anima___ was sure ta___!
4. And it was no___ the shy and quie___ type.
5. I bega___ to ru___!
6. Just then I awoke fro___ my drea___.
7. I'm gla___ I didn't have to see how it ende___!
8. I gue___ I'm reading too many dinosaur book___.

388

4 Final Consonants

Look at the underlined letters in these words:

beef   leak   is   bridge
off   neck
graph   public

What letters can you use to spell the sounds you hear at the end of *sheriff* and *magic*?

What ending letter can stand for the sound you hear at the beginning of *zebra*?

What ending letters can stand for the sound you hear at the beginning of the word *just*?

Read the following story.

My aunt took us to the dock where her sailboat was tied. We had our picnic lunch and some other stuff in canvas bags. When we were ready to go, my brother gave the boat a nudge. It didn't budge. Then he put his legs out and gave a quick kick. We were off! My aunt's scarf blew merrily in the wind. I got a terrific photograph of a bridge. We'd never had half as much fun!

Number your paper from 1 to 4. Write each word below. Next to each word, write the words from the story that end with the same sound.

1. if   **2.** music   **3.** shells   **4.** judge

5 Short Vowels and Graphemic Bases

Read each word in the box below. Look at the underlined letter or letters that spell each short vowel sound.

a	e	i	o	u
th<u>a</u>t	wh<u>e</u>n	k<u>i</u>ck	dr<u>o</u>p	r<u>u</u>n
	w<u>ea</u>lth			

What are two ways to spell the short e vowel sound?

Number your paper from 1 to 12. Read each sentence. Look at the underlined word. Choose the word with the same vowel sound to finish the sentence. Write each sentence on your paper.

1. I found <u>ten</u> _____.   feathers   cans
2. This name <u>tag</u> is for our _____.   puppy   cat
3. She <u>hit</u> the ball with a _____.   bat   stick
4. <u>Tim</u> wanted to _____.   quit   stop
5. The ink in the <u>pen</u> was _____.   red   pink
6. The boy with the <u>drum</u> was _____.   quick   lucky
7. The hair on her <u>head</u> was _____.   wet   thick
8. I do <u>not</u> want to use that _____.   mop   cup
9. We stayed for <u>lunch</u> and _____.   dinner   supper
10. The <u>man</u> was _____.   ready   mad
11. The <u>box</u> was _____.   locked   stuck
12. This <u>bread</u> is _____.   bad   best

390

6 Initial Consonant Clusters

The sounds that letters stand for sometimes blend together. Two or three letters whose sounds blend together are called consonant clusters.

Read the words in the box. Each begins with a consonant cluster.

planet	slipped	broom	twelve	
throw	scratch	straw	sprawled	squint

Number your paper from 1 to 10. Read each word clue. Use one of the consonant clusters in the box below to finish each word.

pl	sl	br	tw	thr	scr	str	spr	squ

1. Add ten and ten to get me.   ___enty
2. I come just before summer.   ___ing
3. Use me with a needle to sew.   ___ead
4. I'm the sound a mouse makes.   ___eak
5. I'm a loud shout or cry.   ___eam
6. I'm never fast.   ___ow
7. I am enough.   ___enty
8. You need me to make a sandwich.   ___ead
9. Hold onto me when you fly a kite.   ___ing
10. You do this when you play ball.   ___ow

391

word work

7 Final Consonant Clusters

Consonant clusters can come at the beginning or at the end of words.

Read the words below. Look at the underlined consonant clusters.

kind servant lamp felt
gold lift   most skunk

Some important ending consonant clusters are listed in the box below.

nd	nt	mp	lt	ld	ft	st	nk

Number your paper from 1 to 8. Copy the sentences below. Use the consonant clusters in the box to fill in the blanks. Use the same consonant cluster for both blanks in a sentence.

1. We had a pleasa___ view of the dista___ mountains.
2. That loud bu___ made me ju___!
3. The touri___ became lo___ in the city.
4. How o___ is that chi___?
5. Was your tru___ on the boat that sa___?
6. I fe___ that his words were an insu___.
7. The ba___ played music from Irela___.
8. Kim le___ her jacket in the haylo___.

8 Long Vowels and Graphemic Bases

The words below show two ways to spell the long *a* vowel sound. Read the words. Look at the underlined letters: t<u>a</u>k<u>e</u>, p<u>ai</u>l.

Read the poem below. As you read, listen for the long *a* vowel sound.

> We went to the station to get Aunt <u>Jane</u>.
> She's afraid of <u>planes</u> and comes by <u>train</u>.
> But <u>rain</u> had <u>made</u> the train quite <u>late</u>.
> We had to wait and wait and <u>wait</u>.

A. Write *a-e* and *ai* at the top of your paper. Write each underlined word from the poem under the heading that spells the long *a* vowel sound the same way.

B. Number your paper from 1 to 8. Read each group of words. Write the two words from each group that have the long *a* vowel sound.

1. crane	**2.** glad	**3.** start	**4.** braids
any	railing	canvas	plate
raisins	wake	parade	bandanna
author	argue	complain	dreary
5. daily	**6.** salami	**7.** fade	**8.** carpet
wear	parsley	fancy	mail
antelope	raincoat	waist	name
mistake	skate	aspen	camera

9 Long Vowels and Graphemic Bases

The long *i* vowel sound can be spelled more than one way. Read the words below. They show two ways to spell the long *i* vowel sound.

sl<u>i</u>d<u>e</u>   dr<u>y</u>

Number your paper from 1 to 24. Read the story below. Then write each word that has a long *i* vowel sound. Underline the letter or letters that stand for the long *i* vowel sound.

One hot day in July, Luis was lying in the grass watching a butterfly in a patch of lupine beside him. He saw Nick ride by on his bike with a package in his hand. Luis asked him what was inside.

"It's my new kite," was his reply. "Do you want to help me fly it?"

"Fine," said Luis, glad that this would satisfy his need for something interesting to do.

It took quite a long time to put it together from a kit. But it sure looked nice when it was done! It was blue with red and white stripes. At last they were ready to try it out. They went to a hillside. It soared like a bird. Soon it was nothing but a little dot in the sky.

10 Long Vowels and Graphemic Bases

The long o vowel sound can be spelled in more than one way. Read the two words below. Look at the underlined letters. They show two ways to spell the long o vowel sound.

envel<u>o</u>pe   mosquit<u>o</u>

Now read this word. The underlined letters spell the long u vowel sound: conf<u>u</u>se.

Number your paper from 1 to 10. Read each sentence and the words that follow it. Write the sentence using the word that has a long o or a long u vowel sound.

1. Cleo liked to play the _____.   banjo   drum
2. Today she was going to play a _____.   song   solo
3. She was going to play in front of the _____ school!   public   whole
4. The stagehand gave her a _____.   cue   nudge
5. She found herself standing on stage _____.   soon   alone
6. The stage seemed _____.   huge   wonderful
7. She _____ she would play well.   hoped   thought
8. What if a string _____?   popped   broke
9. Well, it's no _____ worrying.   fun   use
10. That's always been my _____.   motto   fault

11 Long Vowels and Graphemic Bases

The long e vowel sound can be spelled in more than one way. Read the words below. Look at the underlined letters. They show two ways in which the long e vowel can be spelled.

asl<u>ee</u>p   str<u>ea</u>m

Number your paper from 1 to 10. Read each sentence below. Find the word with the long e vowel sound. Write the long e words on your paper. Underline the letters that stand for this sound.

1. Look at those wonderful seals!
2. It's such fun to watch them dive down deep.
3. They swim around their tank at an astonishing speed.
4. Can you imagine how terrific it would feel to glide through the water like that?
5. What a life they must lead!
6. Is that woman with a bucket going to clean the tank?
7. It seems as if the animals know her.
8. They're barking and splashing a greeting.
9. Oh, now I see why they're so excited.
10. The bucket is full of fish—their favorite treat!

12 Initial and Final Consonant Digraphs

Two or three letters may stand for one sound. Say the words below. Listen for the one sound made by the two or three underlined letters.

<u>ch</u>ur<u>ch</u>   <u>sh</u>y   <u>th</u>ank   <u>wh</u>istle
pa<u>tch</u>   fla<u>sh</u>   wor<u>th</u>

Number your paper from 1 to 13. Read each word clue. Choose letters from those in the box to complete the words.

ch	sh	th	wh	tch

1. I'm what you do when you hurry.   ru___
2. Use me to light a candle.   ma___
3. I'm under something.   benea___
4. You sit on me.   ___air
5. Add ten and twenty to get me.   ___irty
6. I'm part of a tree.   bran___
7. I'm the color of snow.   ___ite
8. You throw me away.   tra___
9. I'm a kind of fish.   ___ark
10. I'm not a fish, but I live in the sea. ___ale
11. I'm right under your mouth.   ___in
12. I'm not fat.   ___in
13. You put me on your feet.   ___oes

397

13 Syllable Generalizations

Learning to divide words into syllables can help you read new words. When you come to a difficult word in your reading, you can work on one small part at a time.

How many vowel sounds do you hear in each word?

| One syllable: | breach | fringe | ought |
| Two syllables: | police | reward | duty |

> Every syllable must have a sounded vowel.

Number your paper from 1 to 8. Say each word below silently. Write **1** if the word has one syllable. Write **2** if it has two syllables.

1. love   **2.** ignore   **3.** moose   **4.** jersey

5. budge   **6.** thought   **7.** degrees   **8.** camel

Below are three words divided into syllables. There is a sounded vowel in each syllable. Notice how the words are divided.

po lice   re ward   du ty

When one consonant is between two vowels, the consonant usually goes with the second syllable.

Number your paper from 1 to 8. Write each word leaving a space between the syllables.

1. cozy   **2.** clover   **3.** label   **4.** lupine

5. paper   **6.** rely   **7.** siren   **8.** bacon

14 Diphthongs

Some vowel combinations make the same sound spelled with different letters.

> sp<u>ou</u>t   fl<u>ow</u>er   sp<u>oi</u>l   destr<u>oy</u>

A. Write *spout* and *spoil* at the top of your paper. Under each word, write the words from the list that have the same vowel sound.

    pounce yowled joyful   moisture scout round
    boil   point   eyebrow annoying toys tower

B. *Ou* and *ow* do not always stand for the vowel sound in *spout*. Six of the words below have the vowel sound you hear in *spout*. Write them on your paper.

    slow   scowled mouth shout crown count
    enough throw   touch could know chow

C. Use letters from the box to make words for each sentence. Write them on your paper.

> ou   ow   oi   oy

1. Joyce fr___ned as she looked d___n at the cloth.
2. How could mother enj___ doing embr___dery?
3. Joyce only f___nd it ann___ing.
4. She wanted to j___n the other kids ___tside.

399

15 *r*-controlled Vowels

The letter *r* changes the sound of the vowel it follows. Some *r*-controlled vowels can be spelled in different ways.

Read the three groups of words below. Listen for the rhyming sounds in each group.

1. sc<u>are</u>   **2.** cl<u>ear</u>   **3.** r<u>oar</u>
   ch<u>air</u>   d<u>eer</u>   f<u>or</u>
            h<u>ere</u>   m<u>ore</u>

The first list shows two ways of spelling the vowel sound you hear in *air*. The second list shows three ways of spelling the vowel sound you hear in *year*. The third list shows three ways of spelling the vowel sound you hear in *store*.

Write the words *air, year,* and *store* at the top of your paper. Under each word, write the six words from the lists below that have the same vowel sound.

soar	stairs	cheer	porch
near	square	story	score
fair	severe	fear	careful
dare	core	veer	royal
earring	mail	fork	beware